A GUIDE TO THE TEMPEST

LISA FABRY

WITH TONY BUZAN

Hodder & Stoughton

Cover photograph ©: Donald Cooper – Photostage
Mind Maps: Philip Chambers
Illustrations: Karen Donnelly

ISBN 0 340 74764 1

First published 1999
Impression number 10 9 8 7 6 5 4 3 2 1
Year 2002 2001 2000 1999

Typeset by Transet Limited, Coventry, England.
Printed in Great Britain for Hodder & Stoughton Educational, a division of Hodder Headline Plc, 338 Euston Road, London NW1 3BH by Cox and Wyman Ltd, Reading, Berks.

CONTENTS

There are five important things you must know about your brain and memory to revolutionize the way you study:

- how your memory ('recall') works *while* you are learning
- how your memory works *after* you have finished learning
- how to use Mind Maps – a special technique for helping you with all aspects of your studies
- how to increase your reading speed
- how to prepare for tests and exams.

Recall during learning

– THE NEED FOR BREAKS

When you are studying, your memory can concentrate, understand and remember well for between 20 and 45 minutes at a time. Then it needs a break. If you carry on for longer than this without a break your memory starts to break down. If you study for hours non-stop, you will remember only a small fraction of what you have been trying to learn, and you will have wasted hours of valuable time.

So, ideally, *study for less than an hour,* then take a five to ten minute break. During the break listen to music, go for a walk, do some exercise, or just daydream. (Daydreaming is a necessary brain-power booster – geniuses do it regularly.) During the break your brain will be sorting out what it has been learning, and you will go back to your books with the new information safely stored and organized in your memory banks. We recommend breaks at regular intervals as you work through the Literature Guides. Make sure you take them!

Recall *after learning*

– THE WAVES OF YOUR MEMORY

What do you think begins to happen to your memory straight after you have finished learning something? Does it immediately start forgetting? No! Your brain actually *increases* its power and carries on remembering. For a short time after your study session, your brain integrates the information, making a more complete picture of everything it has just learnt. Only then does the rapid decline in memory begin, and as much as 80 per cent of what you have learnt can be forgotten in a day.

However, if you catch the top of the wave of your memory, and briefly review (look back over) what you have been studying at the correct time, the memory is stamped in far more strongly, and stays at the crest of the wave for a much longer time. To maximize your brain's power to remember, take a few minutes and use a Mind Map to review what you have learnt at the end of a day. Then review it at the end of a week, again at the end of a month, and finally a week before your test or exam. That way you'll ride your memory wave all the way there – and beyond!

The *Mind Map* ®

– A PICTURE OF THE WAY YOU THINK

Do you like taking notes? More importantly, do you like having to go back over and learn them before tests or exams? Most students I know certainly do not! And how do you take your notes? Most people take notes on lined paper, using blue or black ink. The result, visually, is boring! And what does *your* brain do when it is bored? It turns off, tunes out, and goes to sleep! Add a dash of colour, rhythm, imagination, and the whole note-taking process becomes much more fun, uses more of your brain's abilities, and improves your recall and understanding.

A Mind Map mirrors the way your brain works. It can be used for note-taking from books or in class, for reviewing what you have just studied, and for essay planning for coursework and in tests or exams. It uses all your memory's natural techniques to build up your rapidly growing 'memory muscle'.

You will find Mind Maps throughout this book. Study them, add some colour, personalize them, and then have a go at drawing your own – you'll remember them far better! Stick them in your files and on your walls for a quick-and-easy review of the topic.

HOW TO DRAW A MIND MAP

1 Start in the middle of the page. This gives your brain the maximum room for its thoughts.
2 Always start by drawing a small picture or symbol. Why? Because a picture is worth a thousand words to your brain. And try to use at least three colours, as colour helps your memory even more.
3 Let your thoughts flow, and write or draw your ideas on coloured branching lines connected to your central image. These key symbols and words are the headings for your topic. Start like the Mind Map on page 8.
4 Then add facts and ideas by drawing more, smaller, branches on to the appropriate main branches, just like a tree.
5 Always print your word clearly on its line. Use only one word per line.
6 To link ideas and thoughts on different branches, use arrows, colours, underlining, and boxes (see page 19).

HOW TO READ A MIND MAP

1 Begin in the centre, the focus of your topic.
2 The words/images attached to the centre are like chapter headings; read them next.
3 Always read out from the centre, in every direction (even on the left-hand side, where you will have to read from right to left, instead of the usual left to right).

USING MIND MAPS

Mind Maps are a versatile tool – use them for taking notes in class or from books, for solving problems, for brainstorming with friends, and for reviewing and working for tests or exams – their uses are endless! You will find them invaluable for planning essays for coursework and exams. Number your main branches in the order in which you want to use them and off you go – the main headings for your essay are done and all your ideas are logically organized!

Super speed reading

It seems incredible, but it's been proved – the faster you read, the more you understand and remember! So here are some tips to help you to practise reading faster – you'll cover the ground more quickly, remember more, and have more time left for both work and play.

- First read the whole text (whether it's a lengthy book or an exam or test paper) very quickly, to give your brain an overall idea of what's ahead and get it working. (It's like sending out a scout to look at the territory you have to cover – it's much easier when you know what to expect!) Then read the text again for more detailed information.
- Have the text a reasonable distance away from your eyes. In this way your eye/brain system will be able to see more at a glance, and will naturally begin to read faster.
- Take in groups of words at a time. Rather than reading 'slowly and carefully' read faster, more enthusiastically.
- Take in phrases rather than single words while you read.
- Use a guide. Your eyes are designed to follow movement, so a thin pencil underneath the lines you are reading, moved smoothly along, will 'pull' your eyes to faster speeds.

Preparing for tests and exams

- Review your work systematically. Cram at the start of your course, not the end, and avoid 'exam panic'!
- Use Mind Maps throughout your course, and build a Master Mind Map for each subject – a giant Mind Map that summarizes everything you know about the subject.
- Use memory techniques such as mnemonics (verses or systems for remembering things like dates and events).
- Get together with one or two friends to study, compare Mind Maps, and discuss topics.

AND FINALLY...

Have *fun* while you learn – it has been shown that students who make their studies enjoyable understand and remember everything better and get the highest grades. I wish you and your brain every success!

(Tony Buzan)

How to use this guide

This guide assumes that you have already read *The Tempest,* although you could read 'Background' and 'The story of *The Tempest'* before that. It is best to use this guide alongside the play. You could read 'Who's Who?' and 'Themes' without referring to the play, but you will get more out of these sections if you do refer to it to check the points made in these sections, and especially when tackling the questions designed to test your recall and help you to think about the play.

The sections

The 'Commentary' section can be used in a number of ways. One way is to read a scene or part of a scene in the play, and then read the commentary for that section. Keep on until you come to a test section, test yourself – then have a break! Alternatively, read the Commentary for a scene or part of a scene, then read that scene in the play, then go back to the Commentary. Find out what works best for you.

'Topics for discussion and brainstorming' gives topics that could well feature in exams or provide the basis for coursework. It would be particularly useful for you to discuss them with friends, or brainstorm them using Mind Map techniques (see p. vi).

'How to get an "A" in English Literature' gives valuable advice on what to look for in a text, and what skills you need to develop in order to achieve your personal best.

'The exam essay' is a useful 'night before' reminder of how to tackle exam questions, and 'Model answer' gives an example of an A-grade essay and the Mind Map and plan used to write it.

The questions

Whenever you come across a question in the guide with a star ✪ in front of it, think about it for a moment. You could even jot down a few words in rough to focus your mind. There is not usually a 'right' answer to these questions: it is important for you to develop your own opinions if you want to get an 'A'. The 'Test yourself' sections are designed to take you about

10–20 minutes each – which will be time well spent. Take a short break after each one.

Line numbers

Line references are to the Cambridge School Shakespeare edition. If you have another edition, the line numbers may be slightly different, although the Act and scene numbers will normally be the same.

Key to icons

THEMES

A **theme** is an idea explored by an author. Whenever a theme is dealt with in the guide, the appropriate icon is used. This means you can find where a theme is mentioned just by flicking through the book. Go on – try it now!

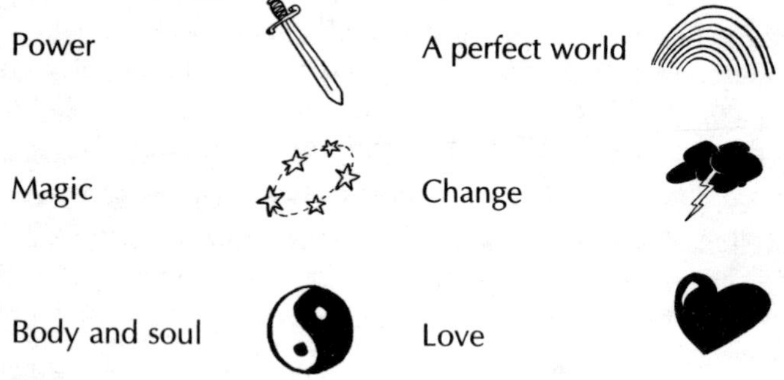

STYLE AND LANGUAGE

This heading and icon are used in the Commentary wherever there is a special section on the author's choice of words and imagery.

BACKGROUND

At one time, people thought that *The Tempest* was one of Shakespeare's earliest plays. We now believe it to be his last play, written in 1610 or 1611. Why do we think this?

The diagram overleaf shows some of the sources which could have influenced Shakespeare. Take time to look at them, they will help you to understand the play's context (how it has been influenced by ideas, events and trends at the time it was written). Although we do not know for sure which ones he read, there are some clues in the play. For example, Shakespeare uses words which are very similar to those in *Metamorphoses, Of the Cannibals* and one of the written accounts of the Bermuda shipwreck. This last source was not written until 1610. The earliest recorded performance of *The Tempest* was in November, 1611.

Two main characters in the play, Prospero and Miranda, travel to a new land and settle there. This reflects events in the early seventeenth century, when people from many European countries travelled to new lands. Some settlers were fleeing persecution; others dreamed of creating an ideal society, or just a better life for themselves. European nations claimed territories for themselves, regardless of who was already living there. In this way they gained huge empires, which lasted into the twentieth century. This kind of settlement is known as 'colonization'. In 1607, the first permanent English settlement in America was set up. In 1608 through to 1610, many English people were sent to colonize Ireland.

The Tempest includes elements of the romance and the masque, two theatrical forms popular in the early seventeenth century. The language in the play is more mature than in Shakespeare's earlier plays (see 'Drama' p. 29).

Take time to look at the diagrams. They will help you to understand the play's context (how it has been influenced by ideas, events and trends at the time it was written). Then try these activities.

- ? Read the plot summary of *The Tempest* on page 2. Highlight any words or phrases that appear in the other summaries on the page.

Possible sources of *The Tempest*

METAMORPHOSES
By Ovid, translated into English by Golding in 1567. An evil witch, Medea, gives up her magic. Her words are echoed by Prospero in Act 5.

THE TEMPEST 1611
A duke, who is also a magician, is deposed (forced from power). He and his daughter escape to an island. Years later a shipwreck during a storm brings their enemies to the island. The magician's daughter falls in love with an enemy's son. The magician regains his dukedom and gives up magic.

CHRONICLE OF WITOLD 1388
A king is deposed and runs away with his daughter.

THE FAIR SIDEA
By Jakob Ayrer (died 1605).
A deposed magician's daughter falls in love with his enemy's son.

OF THE CANNIBALS
By Montaigne, translated into English in 1603; new edition 1610.
A description of New World natives and their society. Themes of free love, shared property and innocence echoed by Gonzalo in Act 2.

WINTER NIGHTS 1609
King Dardanus, a deposed magician, runs away to a Mediterranean setting.

BERMUDA SHIPWRECK 1609
In 1609, the *Sea-Adventure*, the flagship of a fleet headed for America, was wrecked near the coast of Bermuda. The survivors lived on the island for nine months before building a boat to take them to America. Some returned to England in 1610 and published their stories.

Historical background to The Tempest

1558

ELIZABETH I BECOMES QUEEN
Makes Church of England Protestant. Passes laws against Catholics. Fights wars with Ireland from 1593.

1603

ELIZABETH DIES – JAMES I BECOMES KING
Continues war with Ireland.

1605

GUNPOWDER PLOT
Failure of Catholic plot to blow up the King and Parliament.

1607

AMERICAN COLONIZATION
First permanent English settlement established in Virginia.

1608–10

PLANTATION OF ULSTER
English settle (or 'plant') large numbers of people in Ulster, Ireland. Results in divided population: English-speaking Protestant landowners (the settlers), and Gaelic-speaking Catholic underclass (native population).

1609

BERMUDA SHIPWRECK
Nine ships with over 600 passengers set out for the colony of Virginia. One ship is wrecked near Bermuda. The survivors live there for nine months before building their own boat and completing the journey to Virginia.

1611

King James prints the Authorized Version of the Bible, which all people in the Church of England must use.

- ? Make a Mind Map of the themes in *The Tempest* using the information on page 2.
- ? What do you understand by the word 'colonization'? If you're not sure, use a dictionary to help you.

now you understand the background to the play – on with the story

THE STORY OF *THE TEMPEST*

A ship is wrecked during a violent storm at sea and the survivors are washed up on the shore of a remote island. Prospero, a magician, lives on the island with his daughter, Miranda and it is he who has caused the storm. Miranda feels sorry for the people on board the ship and asks her father to calm the storm. Prospero assures Miranda that no one has been hurt and explains why he has caused the storm.

Twelve years ago, he was Duke of Milan. While he was busy studying magic, his wicked brother, Antonio, helped by Alonso, King of Naples, took power, cast Prospero and Miranda out and abandoned them at sea. A friend, Gonzalo, gave them food, water and made sure that Prospero had his magic books – otherwise, they would have died. Prospero and Miranda landed on the island, where they made their home.

On the island, Prospero and Miranda found Caliban, the son of an evil witch, Sycorax, who ruled the island before Prospero. They tried to civilise Caliban by teaching him language. In return, he showed them where to get food and water on the island. But later, he tried to rape Miranda and Prospero punished him by making him a slave. Prospero also found Ariel, a spirit whom Sycorax had imprisoned in a tree. Prospero used his magic to free Ariel. Ariel now serves Prospero, but wants his freedom.

King Alonso's son, Ferdinand, has been washed up on shore alone. Ferdinand believes that his father is dead and that he is now King of Naples. He meets Prospero and Miranda and, as Prospero has planned, the two young people fall in love. In order to test their love, Prospero imprisons Ferdinand and makes him do hard manual labour. Alonso and his followers (including his brother Sebastian, Prospero's brother Antonio and Gonzalo) find themselves in another part of the island. Alonso is grieving for Ferdinand, whom he believes is dead. Gonzalo tries to cheer him up, by reminding him that at least they are alive. Antonio and Sebastian plot to kill Alonso and

Gonzalo while they are asleep, but Ariel wakes them just in time. Stephano, the king's butler and Trinculo, the court jester, meet up with Caliban. Stephano gives Caliban wine and they all get drunk. Caliban calls Stephano a god and promises to serve him. Caliban suggests that they kill Prospero so that Stephano can rule the island. Ariel hears them plotting and reports back to Prospero.

Prospero and Ariel create a magic banquet for Alonso and the other courtiers. Just as they are about to eat, it disappears and Ariel accuses them of overthrowing Prospero. Alonso feels guilty and repents.

Prospero agrees that Ferdinand and Miranda can marry and arranges a masque to celebrate the event. The masque is interrupted when Prospero remembers the plot on his life. He and Ariel lay a trap which ends up with Stephano, Trinculo and Caliban being hunted by a pack of spirit dogs and running away.

Ariel asks Prospero to show mercy towards Alonso and the other courtiers. Prospero explains that he only wanted to use his magic to make them repent, and promises to give up his powers. He allows the courtiers in and reveals himself to them. Alonso begs forgiveness, but Antonio and Sebastian remain unrepentant. Prospero forgives them anyway. Prospero reveals to Alonso that his son is alive. Ferdinand tells his father that he wants to marry Miranda.

Ariel returns with the Master and Boatswain of the ship, who report that the ship is as good as new and that all the sailors have been in a strange sleep aboard.

Caliban, Stephano and Trinculo are brought forward and reprimanded. Caliban is sorry and promises to be good from now on.

Prospero invites the courtiers to stay one night on the island, after which they will all return to Naples together. Prospero asks Ariel for one last service – to make sure they have a good voyage – after which he will be free.

The Tempest – test yourself

? The pictures below tell the story of *The Tempest*. Use them to help you remember the plot.

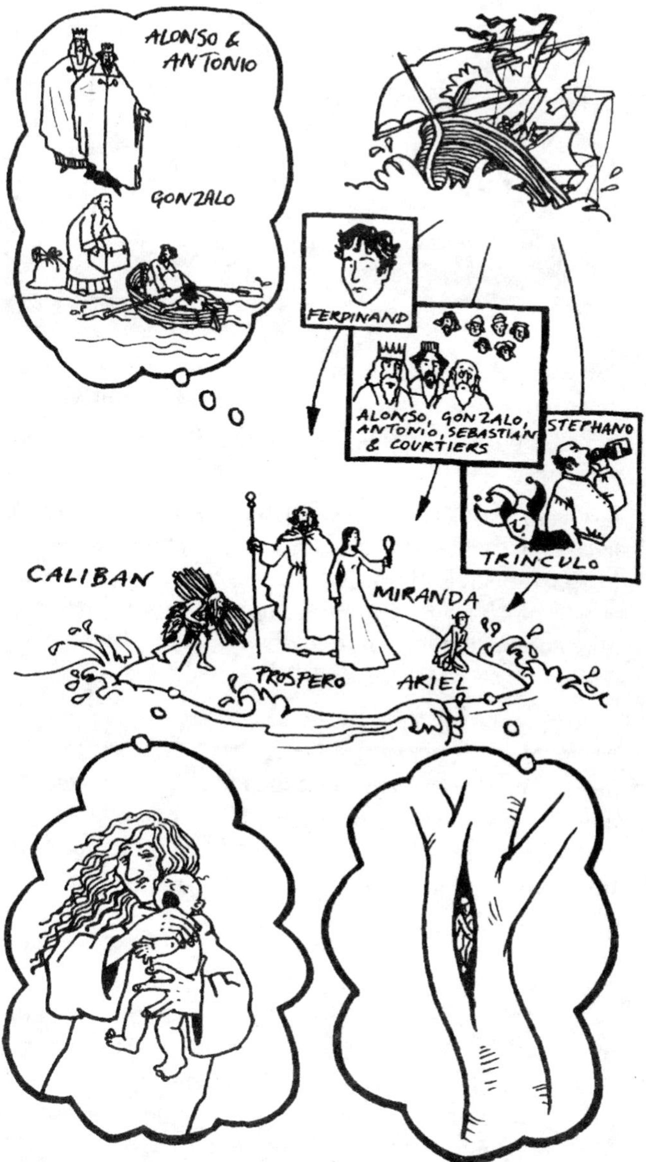

WHO'S WHO?

The Mini Mind Map above summarises the character groups in *The Tempest.* Test yourself by looking at the full Mind Map on p. 21, and then copying the Mini Mind Map and trying to add to it from memory.

Just as in real life, we don't all agree about what people are like, so there have been many interpretations of the characters in Shakespeare's plays. These notes will give you some ideas about the characters in *The Tempest,* but you should read the play and decide for yourself what you think of them.

Prospero

Prospero is a complex character. He has been interpreted in many different ways. Some people have seen him as a kind and wise magician, others as a bitter and cruel man who uses his power to make others do as he wishes.

'A PRINCE OF POWER'

Prospero is the rightful Duke of Milan, wrongly overthrown by his brother Antonio, with the help of Alonso and Sebastian, and exiled on the island. He is a man of learning and reason, who uses the magic he has learned for a good purpose. He wants the people who wronged him to repent, and then he will give up his magical powers:

They being penitent/ The sole drift of my purpose doth extend/ Not a frown further. (Act 5, scene 1, lines 28–30).

Prospero uses his magic gently, not really hurting anyone, either in the storm or on the island. He is a kind and protective father, who has brought up Miranda on his own, educating her and looking after her. As a nobleman, he considers himself the rightful ruler of the island. He tried to civilize Caliban, punishing him only when he tried to rape Miranda. He rescued Ariel from the tree where he had been imprisoned by Caliban's mother, Sycorax, and rewards Ariel with his freedom after he helps Prospero carry out his plan. Some people see Prospero as representing God – good yet fierce. They view the whole play as a Christian **allegory** (a story with a hidden meaning).

'A TYRANT, A SORCERER'

An alternative view of Prospero is that he is a power-mad dictator. Moreover, he is at least partly to blame for losing his dukedom. He was *rapt in secret studies* and neglected his duties, spending all his time reading *volumes that/ I prize above my dukedom.* He allowed Antonio to manage the state, and this *awaked an evil nature* in his brother, who eventually plotted to gain all the power for himself.

Many modern critics have pointed out that Prospero dominates everyone around him. He is kind when people do as he says, but irritable and cruel when his authority is challenged. He orders Miranda about, putting her to sleep when he is fed up with her: *Here cease more questions./ Thou art inclined to sleep* (Act 1, scene 2, lines 184-5). Prospero has stolen the island from Caliban and forced him into slavery. He curses Caliban constantly and uses his magic to torment him physically. Caliban is genuinely frightened of Prospero.

Prospero speaks to Ariel more gently, calling him *brave spirit, fine apparition* and *delicate Ariel.* But in Act 1, scene 2, when Ariel asks for his freedom, Prospero unleashes a stream of abuse, calling him *malignant thing* and threatening to imprison him in a tree again. Ariel begs forgiveness and promises to do as Prospero says. Prospero uses his power over everyone on the island. He imprisons Ferdinand, entrances Alonso and his followers and leads Stephano, Trinculo and Caliban through thorns into a stinking swamp. ✪ Look carefully at the character of Prospero to see which view you are more likely to agree with.

'THE RARER ACTION IS/ IN VIRTUE, THAN IN VENGEANCE'

Towards the end of the play, Prospero acts generously. In Act 4, scene 1 he apologises to Ferdinand and offers him Miranda in marriage. In Act 5, scene 1, Prospero forgives Alonso, Antonio and Sebastian. He frees Ariel and, even though Stephano, Trinculo and Caliban have plotted to kill him, Prospero does not punish them. Finally, he gives up his magical powers. It has been argued that Prospero undergoes a change and learns humility by the end of the play.

Miranda

'O YOU WONDER / O WONDER!'

Miranda's name comes from the Latin, 'to wonder at' or 'wonderful'. Both meanings apply to Miranda.

1 Because Miranda has been brought up on the island, away from society, she is very innocent and **wonders** at every new thing. When she sees all the people from the shipwreck gathered together at the end of the play, she is impressed: *O brave new world/ That has such people in't!* (Act 5, scene 1, lines 183–4).

2 As the only woman in the play, Miranda is seen as **wonderful** and an object of desire. Ferdinand falls instantly in love with her. Caliban has, in the past, tried to have sex with her. Even Stephano plans to make her his queen before he has even seen her.

'SO PERFECT AND SO PEERLESS'

Some people argue that Miranda's character is not fully developed in *The Tempest.* They say that she is a type, representing the perfect woman: compassionate, innocent, obedient and chaste:

- compassionate – she empathizes with the people in the shipwreck, and begs her father not to hurt them:

O I have suffered/ With those that I saw suffer! (Act 1, scene 2, lines 5–6)
- innocent – she takes an innocent delight in the *brave new world* of other human beings, unaware of its faults; she is also innocent in that she commits no selfish or manipulative acts
- obedient – she obeys her father, even when he is irritable with her, for example in Act 1, scene 2, lines 16–186 when Prospero tells her the story of their life
- chaste – she insists on marriage as a condition of her love for Ferdinand (Act 3, scene 1).

However, it could be argued that Miranda does play a more active role. She disobeys her father to speak to Ferdinand, and is forthright and unconventional when she does so, offering to carry logs for him, asking him if he loves her and exacting a promise of marriage. In her simple honesty, she resembles another of Shakespeare's young heroines, Juliet.

Caliban

'A DEVIL...ON WHOSE NATURE/ NURTURE CAN NEVER STICK'

Caliban is described as *a savage and deformed slave.* Savage, because he is wild and uncivilized, like the natives of the Caribbean islands and America, whom Shakespeare would have heard about. Caliban's name might be a play on the words, Carib or cannibal. Deformed, because in Shakespeare's time a physical handicap was thought to indicate an evil nature.

In Prospero's opinion, Caliban is naturally bad. His mother was an evil witch, and therefore Caliban must be wicked as well. Despite Prospero's efforts to educate Caliban, he is still governed by instinct rather than reason. He is both lustful – he attempted to rape Miranda; and lazy – he has to be forced to do the work that Prospero sets him. (Remember some **caLL** **CaL**iban **L**ustful and **L**azy.)

When Stephano gives him wine, Caliban thinks he is a god and kneels to him. It has been argued that Caliban is a fool, willing to worship anyone who comes along.

'THIS ISLAND'S MINE'

Modern critics have been more likely to view Caliban as a victim of colonization. Caliban sees himself as the rightful ruler of the island, because his mother, Sycorax, was there before Prospero. He accuses Prospero of stealing the island from him. Caliban has an affinity with the natural setting of the island that no other character has. He understands its moods and noises, and knows where to find food and water. Caliban's descriptions of the island use some of the most beautiful language in the play. Caliban shared his knowledge of the island with Prospero, only to be enslaved by him. Yet, during the play, he is willing to give the same information to Stephano, and become his subject instead.

People who support this view say that Caliban is not a fool – in Act 4, scene 1 he recognises that Stephano and Trinculo are foolish for being distracted by the gaudy clothes Prospero and Ariel have displayed. Neither is he hungry for power, he just wants his freedom, and is willing to play along with anyone who he thinks might be able to help him.

Ariel

'I COME/ TO ANSWER THY BEST PLEASURE'

Ariel is, for the most part, Prospero's willing servant. He serves Prospero because the magician released him from the cloven pine tree where he was imprisoned by Sycorax. His manner is light, happy and eager to please. Ariel carries out Prospero's commands with little effort and no mistakes. It is Ariel who performs the magic that brings on the 'tempest' which gives the play its title, leads Ferdinand to Miranda and presents the courtiers with a false banquet. Ariel also supplies the music that is such a big part of the play.

Prospero seems to love Ariel, speaking to him affectionately, calling him *bird, brave spirit,* and *delicate Ariel.* Ariel enjoys this attention, asking: *Do you love me master?* (Act 4, scene 1, line 48) and *Was't well done?* (Act 5, scene 1, line 240).

'MALIGNANT THING'

Prospero's affection soon turns to anger when Ariel asks for his freedom, in the middle of Act 1, scene 2. Prospero turns on Ariel, abusing him and threatening to punish him. Ariel apologises and promises to be good in future. Some critics say that the relationship between Prospero and Ariel is like father and child. When Prospero is affectionate, Ariel is happy and eager to please. When Prospero is angry, Ariel becomes sullen and apologetic. If this is a father-child relationship, Prospero is a very old-fashioned father, expecting instant obedience and punishing any disobedience.

Other people have likened this relationship to that of a master and slave. Unlike Caliban, Ariel plays the role of the willing servant, in order to get what he wants. He and Prospero are affectionate towards each other but this does not hide the fact that Ariel is Prospero's slave.

'THY THOUGHTS I CLEAVE TO'

Ariel is a spirit invisible to everyone in the play except Prospero. Some people have seen Ariel as a part of Prospero's imagination. He only has to think of Ariel and the spirit appears: *Come with a thought!* (Act 4, scene 1, line 164). Having Ariel means that Prospero can tell the audience what he is thinking and planning, without using a lot of **soliloquies** (speeches spoken while alone on stage).

'AIRY SPIRIT'

Ariel is a spirit, so is neither man nor woman. In contrast to Caliban's very male sexuality, Ariel is asexual (without sex). In the stage directions, Ariel is described as 'he' and in early productions, Ariel would always have been played by a male actor. But for a long time, between the 18th and early 20th centuries, a female actor usually played the part. Nowadays, it varies. All the roles that Ariel takes within the play (harpy, nymph, Ceres) are female, but this fits in with Shakespeare's theatre where boy actors took female roles.

Alonso

'WHAT CARE THESE ROARERS FOR THE NAME OF KING?'

In Shakespeare's time the king was the most important person, next to God. But when we first meet Alonso, it is on board ship in the middle of the tempest. Alonso's traditional authority is challenged by the Boatswain, who says that the storm does not care whether someone is a king or not, and insists that the King and his courtiers stay out of the way and let the mariners do their job.

'WISELY...WEIGH OUR SORROW WITH OUR COMFORT'

The next time we meet Alonso, he has been washed up on shore the island. He believes his son Ferdinand is dead and he is weak with grief. Gonzalo tries to cheer him up, urging him to weigh up the good things against the bad. Alonso refuses to listen to Gonzalo. ✪ Do you think it makes sense that Alonso is so depressed, or should a king keep his personal feelings to himself?

'THREE MEN OF SIN'

Alonso, Sebastian and Antonio were responsible for overthrowing Prospero. In Act 3, scene 3, when Ariel, in the role of a harpy, accuses them, Alonso is the only one to be overcome by guilt. Antonio and Sebastian draw their swords against the harpy, but Alonso believes that the death of his son, Ferdinand, is his punishment for sinning against Prospero and rushes away, threatening to commit suicide.

'THY DUKEDOM I RESIGN, AND DO ENTREAT/ THOU PARDON ME MY WRONGS'

Earlier in the play, Ariel sings to Ferdinand about his father, saying that he is undergoing a 'sea-change'. Alonso is the character who changes the most in the play. By the end, he begs Prospero's forgiveness, and is rewarded with seeing his son alive again.

Antonio and Sebastian

'EXPELLED REMORSE AND NATURE'

Antonio is Prospero's brother, who plotted to overthrow him and exile him from Milan. He has committed one of the worst sins: betraying his own family. This, according to Shakespeare, is going against nature. Worse, he seems to have no remorse for what he has done. Sebastian is Alonso's brother, as evil and unrepentant as Antonio.

'HANG, CUR, HANG'

Antonio and Sebastian are shown to be nasty pieces of work right from the beginning of the play. In Act 1, scene 1, they curse the Boatswain unnecessarily violently, and accuse the mariners of being drunkards. In Act 2, scene 1, when they are washed up on the island, they make cruel fun of Gonzalo, pouring scorn on his attempts to cheer up the king. Their words are witty, but it is a cruel and sarcastic humour.

'AS THOU GOT'ST MILAN,/ I'LL COME BY NAPLES'

In Act 2, scene 1 Antonio suggests that Sebastian murder Alonso while he sleeps, and thus become King of Naples. Sebastian does not take long to agree with this plan and Alonso is only saved because Ariel wakes Gonzalo, who in turn, wakes the King.

'I DO FORGIVE/ THY RANKEST FAULT'

Even by the end of the play, Antonio and Sebastian do not repent. Yet Prospero forgives them anyway. ✪ Why do you think Shakespeare makes Antonio and Sebastian unrepentant?

Ferdinand

'A THING DIVINE'

Many people see Ferdinand as the handsome prince of the story. If Miranda is the perfect woman, Ferdinand is the perfect man. When Miranda first sees him, she thinks he is a spirit. (because she has seen no one else except Prospero and

Caliban since she was two). Her father tells her that Ferdinand is only human, but Miranda is besotted and calls him *a thing divine* (Act 1, scene 2, line 417). Ferdinand is similarly taken with Miranda and calls her a goddess. It is Prospero's plan that the two young people fall in love, but he keeps this a secret from Miranda and Ferdinand. Prospero makes Ferdinand move thousands of logs, to test his love for Miranda. Ferdinand tells Miranda that he is willing to do the task to prove how much he loves her: *For your sake/ Am I this patient log-man.* (Act 3, scene 1, lines 68–9).

'MYSELF AM NAPLES'

Ferdinand believes his father is dead in the shipwreck and, although he is sad, he takes on the duty of being the new king immediately, introducing himself to Prospero and Miranda as the King of Naples. ✪ Compare this behaviour with that of Alonso earlier in the scene.

'THERE'S NOTHING ILL CAN DWELL IN SUCH A TEMPLE'

Miranda believes that Ferdinand must be a good person because he is so handsome. Prospero pretends not to be impressed by Ferdinand. He tells her:

> *Thou think'st there is no more such shapes as he,*
> *Having seen but him and Caliban. Foolish wench,*
> *To th'most of men this is a Caliban,*
> *And they to him are angels.*
> (Act 1, scene 2, lines 477–80)

Miranda tells Prospero that she does not want anything better, Ferdinand is good enough for her. ✪ Is Miranda right to do this, or can you see any good sense in Prospero's words?

Gonzalo

'AN HONEST OLD COUNCILLOR'

Gonzalo is described as *honest, honourable* and *noble.* He was kind to Prospero and Miranda when they were cast out of Milan and he is loyal and protective to his king, Alonso. In the first scene he tries to calm the angry Boatswain and remind him that he has the king on board. In Act 2, scene 1, he tries to comfort Alonso over the loss of Ferdinand. Later in the scene, it is Gonzalo's first thought to protect Alonso, when he wakes and finds Antonio and Sebastian with swords drawn. Throughout the play, it is Gonzalo who always finds something good to say about the situation. On board ship, he takes comfort from the idea that the Boatswain looks as if he will die by hanging rather than drowning. On the island, he gives thanks that they are alive and imagines the island to be a perfect world. At the end of the play, he rejoices that things have turned out so well for everyone.

'WHAT A SPENDTHRIFT IS HE OF HIS TONGUE'

In Act 2, scene 1 Antonio accuses Gonzalo of talking too much, and Alonso asks him to be quiet several times. Gonzalo does talk a lot, and critics have said that he is falsely optimistic, especially at the end of the play (Act 5, scene 1, lines 205–13). ✪ Do you think that Gonzalo is wise and kind, or is he a bit of a fool?

Adrian and Francisco

Adrian and Francisco are part of Alonso's royal party. They do not have much to say in the play. Most of their lines are in Act 2, scene 1, where they lend support to Gonzalo's optimistic view of the situation. They appear in later scenes, but apart from one line for Francisco, they do not say anything. Shakespeare might have included these characters to 'pad out' the royal party, or he might have wanted to balance the *three men of sin* (Alonso, Sebastian and Antonio) with three good men (Gonzalo, Adrian and Francisco), or he could have had some other reason. ✪ What purpose do you think they serve?

Stephano and Trinculo

Stephano, the butler and Trinculo, the jester are lowlife rebels whose drunken exploits provide comic relief. Their characters contrast both with Caliban and with the nobility in the play.

Their plan to kill Prospero mirrors the main plot. Stephano is drunk throughout the play. He is a fool, who is as taken in by Caliban as Caliban is by him. When Caliban offers him the chance to kill Prospero and become king, he is intrigued by the idea, but in the end he is just too drunk and lazy to carry out the plan. Trinculo is just as drunken and foolish as Stephano, but he does offer some words of wisdom in the play. In Act 2, scene 2 he remarks that Caliban is a fool to worship a drunk and in Act 3, scene 2, he comments ironically on everything the others say.

The ship's crew

The Master of the ship is more important than the Boatswain, but he has only a few lines. The Boatswain plays the biggest part of all the mariners. We see him first on board ship, in the middle of the tempest. He is a working man, trying to do his job under difficult conditions. He tries to be polite to the noblemen getting in his way, but soon loses his temper and begins to curse them. His authority on the ship overrides the traditional hierarchy where the king is in charge, and the noblemen have to do as he says.

The other mariners demonstrate the ferocity of the storm, as we see them battling against it, trying, and failing, to save the ship. The Master and the Boatswain appear again at the end of the play. Again, it is the Boatswain who speaks, reporting on the ship and its crew, without a trace of the anger we saw earlier.

Who's who?

? Fill in the correct answer:
Who said, *This island's mine?* ______________
Who is described as *a thing divine*? ______________
Whose name means 'wonderful'? ______________
Who plays the role of a harpy? ______________
Who are the *three men of sin*? ______________

take a break before moving on to the themes

SEBASTIAN
ANTONIO
TRINCULO
STEPHANO
ADRIAN
FRANCISCO
LORDS
NO BIL ITY
WOR KER S
GONZALO
ALONSO
FERDINAND
MASTER
BOATSWAIN
OTHER MARINERS
MARINERS
PROSPERO
ISLANDERS
MIRANDA
ARIEL
CALIBAN

THEMES

A **theme** is an idea developed or explored throughout a work. The main themes of *The Tempest* are shown in picture form in the Mini Mind Map above. Test yourself by looking at the full Mind Map on p. 28, and then copying the Mini Mind Map and trying to add to it from memory.

Change

At the centre of the play is the theme of change. The tempest is the symbol for this change. A storm brings change to the natural world. Before a storm, the atmosphere may feel close and uncomfortable. A storm, though it may be violent and damaging, clears the air and brings a feeling of freshness and renewal. In *The Tempest,* order has been upset by the overthrow of Prospero. The storm brings the people responsible to the island so that they can be given the chance to repent for their sins, Prospero can reclaim his rightful place and order can be restored.

The storm is both the literal cause of the events in the play and a **metaphor** for the transformation (an emotional, psychological, and even spiritual 'tempest') that the characters undergo. The importance of the tempest as a symbol is shown by the fact that Shakespeare uses it as the title for the play.

Change occurs in several ways in the play. You could remember these as the **Three Rs**:

- **Repentance** – Prospero's only aim is to make the people who wronged him sorry for what they did: *They being penitent,/ The sole drift of my purpose doth extend/ Not a frown further.* (Act 5, scene 1, lines 28–30)
- **Renunciation** – Prospero renounces magical power in order to regain civil power as the Duke of Milan: *this rough magic/ I here abjure* (Act 5, scene 1, lines 50–1). Alonso renounces all claim to Prospero's dukedom: *Thy dukedom I resign, and do entreat/ Thou pardon me my wrongs.* (Act 5, scene 1, lines 118–19).
- **Reconciliation** – By the end of the play, Prospero and Alonso are reconciled. The marriage of Miranda and Ferdinand seals this reconciliation. Ariel is free and Caliban has promised to *seek for grace.*

? Who changes during the play? ? Who does not change?

Power

The play shows us power in many forms:

- kings and dukes over their states and subjects
- fathers over their children
- masters over their slaves and servants
- sailors over their crew and passengers

In Shakespeare's time, the hierarchy of power was very rigid, and people were not expected to challenge their superiors. For example, a king was considered to be second only to God in power. On the domestic front, wives and daughters were expected to obey the man of the house. In *The Tempest,* characters continually challenge authority:

- Antonio, Sebastian and Alonso overthrow Prospero
- the Boatswain overrides the power of the king
- Caliban challenges Prospero's right to the island
- Ariel demands his freedom
- Antonio and Sebastian attempt to kill Alonso
- Miranda disobeys her father to speak to Ferdinand
- Stephano, Trinculo and Caliban plot to kill Prospero.

These challenges remind us that relationships where one person has power over another are unstable. There is always the possibility that the person being controlled will rebel and seize power or demand freedom.

Another question the play raises is: Who uses power wisely and who abuses it? As you have already seen, opinions vary over Prospero's use of his power. Some people think he uses it to achieve good, while others accuse him of unjustly oppressing others. ✪ What do you think?

Magic

Closely linked to the theme of power is the theme of magic. The play is full of magic. The island is an enchanted, dreamy place, full of spirits, visions and strange sounds (see Caliban's description in Act 3, scene 2, lines 130–8). Before Prospero, or even Sycorax, arrived on the island, it was inhabited by Ariel and the other spirits. Then Sycorax came, pregnant with Caliban. She was a witch, who brought evil magic to the island. We never hear exactly what she did, only that there were *mischiefs manifold, and sorceries terrible* (Act 1, scene 2, line 264), and that her *earthy and abhorred commands* were too dreadful for delicate Ariel to carry out, so she imprisoned him in a cloven pine tree. Many critics argue that Prospero's magic is good, in contrast with the evil magic of Sycorax.

In Shakespeare's time, magic was linked to philosophy, science and religion. Even the king at the time *The Tempest* was written (James I) was interested in magic and had written a book about it. Prospero has learned his magic from books; it is an 'art' that he has studied, in order to control the natural world. Ironically, it was his devotion to learning about magic that led to him losing his civil power and later, it is this magic that helps him to regain his dukedom. Prospero's magic has its limits. He relies on the help of Ariel, and fate. For example, it was *providence divine* which ensured that he and Miranda landed safely on the island, and *bountiful Fortune* which brought his enemies within reach. Prospero's powers are greater than those of Sycorax. We hear this from Caliban:

I must obey; his art is of such power,
It would control my dam's god Setebos,
And make a vassal of him.
(Act 1, scene 2, lines 372–4)

Prospero keeps Caliban in line by causing him to suffer cramps and pains. He ensures Ariel's obedience by threatening to imprison him again for another 12 years. ✪ Is this 'good' magic?

Prospero's magic is represented by his magic garments, his staff and, most importantly, his books. It is these magic books that Gonzalo ensures Prospero has when he is cast out of Milan. Caliban knows that without his books, Prospero is powerless and tells Stephano three times in Act 3, scene 2 that all he needs to do in order to get the better of Prospero is to deprive him of his books. At the end of the play, Prospero gives up his magical powers to reclaim his civil power. He changes out of his magic garment and puts on his hat and rapier (symbols of civil power). He promises:

I'll break my staff
Bury it certain fathoms in the earth,
And deeper than did ever plummet sound
I'll drown my book.
(Act 5, scene 1, lines 54–7)

We do not, however, see Prospero do this. It is left to the audience to decide whether he really does give up his magic!

Another kind of 'magic' is theatrical illusion. One view of Prospero is that he represents Shakespeare himself. Prospero can be seen as a theatre director who manages the events of the plot and commands the actors. Many of Prospero's magic feats are theatrical and the language of the play reflects this. For example, in Act 4, scene 1, lines 146–63, Prospero uses the following theatrical images:

- *revels*
- *insubstantial pageant*
- *actors*
- *baseless fabric* (like scenery)
- *rack* (stage clouds painted on scenery).

Because *The Tempest* is probably the last play Shakespeare wrote, apart from a couple of later collaborations, people argue that Prospero's renunciation of his magic represents Shakespeare's farewell to the stage. ✪ Do you agree?

Magical imagery

? The words below, from Act 1, scene 2, all have something to do with magic. Choose any other scene in the play and write down all the words that conjure up images of magic, sleep, dreams, strange happenings or theatrical illusion.

art magic strange asleep spiriting apparition spirit amazement dream mischiefs charm sorceries invisible sprites power

take a break from the supernatural, and come back refreshed in body and soul

Body and soul

Body and soul is a convenient phrase to remind yourself of the contrast in *The Tempest* between the world of reality and instinct and the world of the spirit and imagination.

The **body** represents earthly values such as greed, ambition, sexuality and vengeance. The visitors to the island are greedy for food, drink and power. When Alonso and his followers are offered a feast, they are eager to eat it, only to discover it is an illusion. Stephano and Trinculo drink far too much and make fools of themselves. Antonio and Sebastian are ambitious for power.

The character most associated with the body is Caliban. Prospero even calls him *thou earth* (Act 1, scene 2, line 315), linking him with earthly, not spiritual, qualities. He is governed by his instinct. In the past he attempted to rape Miranda and shows no signs of remorse. His only regret is that he did not manage to do it. Caliban's instinctive sexuality could be seen as evil, or it could be seen as the natural expression of a creature from a world without rules and morals.

Prospero too, has his earthly vices. He is consumed by anger at the wrong done to him by Antonio, Sebastian and Alonso, and he cannot wait to get his revenge.

The **soul** is associated with the imagination, with thoughts and dreams. Prospero is a man of learning, who uses his reason to guide his actions. In Act 5, scene 1, he decides that even though he feels anger towards his enemies, he will be merciful. He uses his *nobler reason* to control his instinctive *fury*. In the same way, Ferdinand, though he is strongly attracted to Miranda, promises to control his feelings of lust. In both these cases, it is a triumph of soul over body.

If the body is represented by the earth and Caliban, the soul is represented by the air and Ariel. Ariel is *an airy spirit*, who is not limited by an earthly body. He can *fly, swim, dive into the fire* and *ride on curled clouds*. As a spirit, Ariel is not supposed to have human feelings. In Act 5, scene 1 he says his *affections would become tender...were I human*. Although he says this, we are not sure whether to believe him. Despite his invisibility and lack of an earthly body, Ariel does seem to express various emotions, such as hurt, pity and resentment.

Make a Mind Map to help you remember some of the associations with body and soul. Use colour and pictures or symbols to make the Mind Map more memorable.

A perfect world

The world that Shakespeare shows us in his plays is not perfect. It is full of ambitious, lustful and greedy people. Even the good characters usually have some flaws. But he seems to be haunted by the idea that a perfect world could exist. How does he show this?

Shakespeare often presents contrasting values, for example, nature versus civilization, or the body versus the soul. He shows there are good and bad points to each side and seems to say that if we could only achieve a mixture of the good points, then we could achieve a balance, a synthesis (joining of two or more parts), a union – a perfect world.

In *The Tempest* the island represents the world of nature. The visitors from the outside world represent civilization. Nature is good when it is bountiful, fertile and under control. It is bad when instinct and sexuality are given free reign. Civilization is good when it represents learning, duty and the ability to control nature. It is bad when it brings about selfish ambition, greed and betrayal. For example, Prospero represents good civilisation through his learning and ability to control nature; and Antonio shows the bad side, through his betrayal of his brother to further his ambition. Miranda, through her compassion and potential fertility, shows all that is good about nature, while Caliban, with his uncontrolled lust, demonstrates its bad side.

The masque in Act 4, scene 1 is Prospero's vision of a perfect world. The masque is to bless the marriage of Ferdinand and Miranda, which will unite Milan and Naples. Ceres, the goddess of the harvest, represents the bounty and fertility of the earth. Venus and Cupid, who represent the bad side of nature, sex, are barred from the masque. Juno, the queen of the gods, represents the heavens. Iris is the goddess of rainbow. The rainbow appears after a storm, bringing calm. Its shape links the heavens and the earth, symbolising peace and union. See p. 31 in Drama for more on the masque.

Love

There are several types of love in the play: paternal love, given by fathers to their children, or masters to their servants; child-like love given in return; romantic love; sexual love; and brotherly or friendly love.

Prospero has a variety of relationships in the play. He can be seen as a father figure not only to Miranda, but to Caliban and Ariel as well. He is kind and caring towards Miranda, though he expects her to be obedient and is impatient when she shows any spirit of her own. Similarly, Prospero is affectionate towards Ariel but his love turns to rage when his authority is questioned. We hear that Prospero was kind to Caliban when he first came to the island but if he ever did love Caliban, this feeling has completely gone, to be replaced with disgust and cruelty.

Prospero's 'children' return their love in different ways. Miranda is passive and obedient, but she consciously disobeys her father to talk to Ferdinand. Ariel is like a small child, eager to please and desperate for approval, responding to Prospero's praise by showing off and being excited, and to his criticism and threats by being sullen and fearful. Caliban tells Prospero that he remembers a time in the past when Prospero was kind to him, and tells him: *And then I loved thee* (Act 1, scene 2, line 337). Now, he responds to Prospero's cruel treatment with curses and reluctance to work.

The love between Miranda and Ferdinand is 'love at first sight' – pure romantic love. Prospero, however, constantly warns Ferdinand against giving way to lust, even though Ferdinand seems to act like a perfect gentleman. ✪ Why do you think he does this? As the only woman in the play, Miranda is the target for a lot of attention: Caliban tries to rape her; Stephano wants to make her his bride; Ferdinand loves her; and Prospero cares for her and controls her.

If Prospero comes across as bitter and cross in the play, it may be because of how he was betrayed by his brother Antonio: *he, whom next thyself/ Of all the world I loved* (Act 1, scene 2, lines 68–9). The brotherly love he felt in the past was abused, and this might make him less likely to trust people now.

Lastly, there is the love between friends. The love of Gonzalo for both Prospero and Alonso seems to be genuine. Gonzalo was kind to Prospero and Miranda when they were exiled from Milan and Prospero remembers Gonzalo with respect and affection. Gonzalo shows concern for Alonso throughout the play, and tries to protect and cheer him. Alonso, however, often seems impatient with Gonzalo. ✪ How far do you feel this is because he is grieving over Ferdinand, and how far do you feel there are other reasons?

now take a well deserved break

Magic
POWER
a Perfect World
Love
CHANGE
Body &
Soul

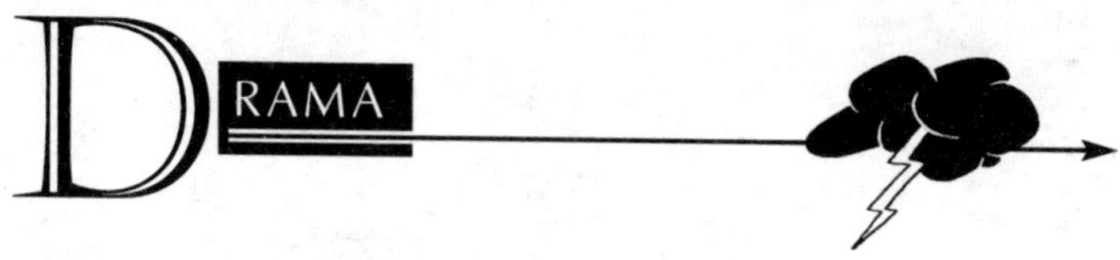

The Mini Mind Map above shows some areas to think about when studying a Shakespeare play. Look at the full Mind Map on p. 36 to see how these relate to *The Tempest*, then copy the Mini Mind Map on this page and add to it from memory.

Performance

It might seem obvious, but *The Tempest* is a play. It was written to be performed on stage and watched by an audience. It will help you enormously to see a performance of *The Tempest*. If you can't get to a live performance, you might be able to see it on video. While you are studying the play, you will probably have a printed copy of the text, which you may read silently to yourself. As you do this, make a real effort to imagine the play in performance, thinking about the points below. Many of the activities in this guide will help you to do this. It will help you to understand the play and you should get higher marks if you refer to the play's dramatic qualities in your essays. These are some of the areas you should keep in mind:

- **Theatre** – Shakespeare's plays have been performed in all kinds of theatres, with varying styles of scenery, costume, lighting, sound and special effects. Compare the Elizabethan theatre above with a modern theatre you have been to. Brainstorm a list of differences. What effect do you think these differences could have on a performance of *The Tempest*?
- **Director** – Productions vary considerably, depending on the **interpretation** (understanding of the meaning). The director will have his or her interpretation and will develop this through working with the actors.
- **Actors** – Working with the director, actors add their own interpretation of characters and events in the play. Their performance (body language, tone of voice, facial expression, gesture) can add meaning to the text.
- **Language and structure** – Some productions stick faithfully to the original text. Some leave out awkward or lengthy passages, or modernise the language. Others alter the order in which scenes occur. Changes like these can affect how the audience understands the play. For example, in Act 1, scene 2, lines 351–62 are Miranda's in the original text, but for many years they were given to Prospero because editors and directors thought they were too harsh for Miranda.

Genre

THE ROMANCE

Shakespeare wrote four types, or genres of plays:

- comedies
- tragedies
- histories
- romances.

The Tempest is a romance. Romances were a popular genre at the beginning of the 17th century. Shakespeare's other romances are *Pericles, Cymbeline* and *The Winter's Tale.*
✪ Look at the following features of romances and think about how they relate to *The Tempest.*

Romances...

- Focus on life's big questions, not individual problems.
- Involve characters who are types, rather than individuals.
- Concern noble families, whose lives are disrupted, are often separated for many years, and are reunited at the end.
- Take place in an unrealistic world, full of make-believe and magic.
- Combine some elements of comedy and some of tragedy. The events in romances seem to lead towards tragedy but there is usually a sudden turn of events which leads to a happy ending.
- Portray the possibility of a perfect world, the result of a synthesis (union) between opposing values

THE MASQUE

Another popular genre at the time when *The Tempest* was written was the **masque**. Masques were short plays, usually allegories, performed at court. The plays involved music, dance, spectacular effects and scenery. The lords and ladies of the court, even the monarch, often joined in the masque. Shakespeare includes a masque in Act 4, scene 1, and it has been said that the whole of the play is influenced by the masque, relying as it does on music, song and special effects.

Structure

Like Shakespeare's other plays, *The Tempest* is presented in five acts. In the first act, the situation is explained and most of the characters are introduced. In the second act, problems arise. In the third act, problems are intensified, coming to a crisis in Act 4. In the final act, the situation is resolved.

Unlike most of Shakespeare's other plays, *The Tempest* adheres to the **dramatic unities**. These are conventions of drama, established by the ancient Greeks. There are three unities:

- time – the action of the play takes place within a day;
- action – all the action relates directly to the main plot;
- place – the action of the play takes place in one location.

TIME

The action covers about four hours. The past is not shown, only referred to in Prospero's story as *the dark backward and abysm of time* (Act 1, scene 2, line 50). Because there is so little time for Prospero to carry out his plan, he uses devices which have the effect of slowing time down. He puts Miranda to sleep. He also uses Ariel to put Alonso and Gonzalo to sleep, to charm Caliban, Stephano and Trinculo and lead them into a swamp and to confine all the courtiers in a grove of trees. Later, Prospero keeps the courtiers in a trance on stage until he is ready for them. These events show Prospero's magic powers and they also buy him time.

ACTION

All the action in the play relates to the main plot: Prospero's revenge and reinstatement as the Duke of Milan. Unlike some other Shakespeare plays, where the subplots are stories in themselves, the subplots in *The Tempest*: Sebastian and Antonio plotting to murder Alonso; Caliban, Stephano and Trinculo plotting to murder Prospero; and the courtship of Ferdinand and Miranda are all directly linked to the main plot.

PLACE

All the action of the play takes place on or near the island. The setting is not a real place. It should be in the Mediterranean, if

Alonso's ship is on its way back from Tunis to Italy. But the island has some of the qualities of the New World that Shakespeare would have heard about: rugged, wild and uncivilized. The island is an unreal world, a place in the imagination.

Language

Dramatic language is quite different from the language used in novels. For one thing, there is no description. Everything must be said by characters, either to themselves (soliloquy), in conversation (dialogue) or as a speech to other, silent, characters (dramatic monologue).

Shakespeare writes in prose and verse. Prose is usually used by commoners, while the nobility speak in **blank** (non-rhyming) **verse**. There are exceptions to this. Higher status characters often use prose when being informal or humorous. Some lower status characters speak in verse. In *The Tempest*, Caliban is given some of the most beautiful poetry in the play. This could be because he was taught language by a nobleman, Prospero, or it could be to show his sensitivity to nature and music, or there could be another reason. ✪ Study Caliban's lines carefully to see what you think.

The Tempest is thought to be Shakespeare's last play. Critics say that the language shows the maturity of his later plays. What do they mean by this? These are some of the features of Shakespeare's mature language, focusing on Prospero's language in Act 1, scene 2.

- **Irregular rhythm** – instead of a regular **iambic pentameter**, with the meaning contained within each line, the rhythm is irregular, more like real speech, and the meaning flows over the ends of lines:

  Knowing I loved my books, he furnished me
  From mine own library, with volumes that
  I prize above my dukedom.
  (lines 166–8)
- **Vivid and concise description** – using fewer words to create meaningful images:

he needs will be/ Absolute Milan (lines 108–9) – 'he felt that he had to gain all the power over Milan for himself'
thy crying self (line 132) – 'you, who were crying at the time'
an undergoing stomach (line 157) – 'the ability to endure difficulties'

- **Contractions** – missing parts of words. For example in lines 79–87, Prospero uses the following contractions: *t'advance, changed 'em, new formed 'em, I'th'state, on't, attend'st.* This shows the urgency of Prospero to tell his story. There is so much to tell and there is so much emotion involved that the words tumble out on top of each other.
- **Hyphenated words** – the play is full of words linked in this way, which seem to create new meanings. Examples in this scene include: *over-topping, o'er-prized, hag-born, ever-angry, hag-seed, fresh-brook, sea-sorrow.*
- **Repetition of phrases, words, sounds and images** – for example, the extensive use of alliteration: *prince of power, noble Neapolitan, secret studies.*
- **Few rhyming couplets (two rhyming lines)** – in his early plays, such as *Romeo and Juliet,* Shakespeare used lots of rhyming couplets, often at the end of a scene. Because rhyming couplets are not like real speech, they remind the audience that they are watching a play. In *The Tempest,* Shakespeare uses very few rhyming couplets, sticking to more realistic language.

Dramatic irony is when the audience knows something that a character does not. For example, when Miranda sees Alonso and the courtiers for the first time she says, *How many goodly creatures are there here!/ How beauteous mankind is!* We know that the group she is admiring includes Alonso, Antonio and Sebastian, who have behaved very badly, and we realize the irony of her statement.

Imagery is the use of language to create vivid sense impressions – pictures, sounds, feelings or smells – in your mind. Shakespeare uses different kinds of imagery, including metaphor, simile, personification and comparisons. Many of the images in *The Tempest* relate to the themes outlined earlier in the guide, for example magic.

Appeal to your senses

? Your senses will help you to remember the play. Choose one of the examples of imagery below. Read it and look up the section of the play from which it comes. Which senses does the passage appeal to? Draw a picture of the image the words conjure up. Look out for others as you read the play.

he was
The ivy which had hid my princely trunk,
And sucked my verdure out on't
(Act 1, scene 2, lines 85–7)

I saw him beat the surges under him,
And ride upon their backs;
(Act 2, scene 1, lines 109–10)

They'll take suggestions as a cat laps milk;
(Act 2, scene 1, line 281)

sometime am I
All wound with adders, who with cloven tongues
Do hiss me into madness.
(Act 2, scene 2, lines 12–14)

take a break, then on with the play!

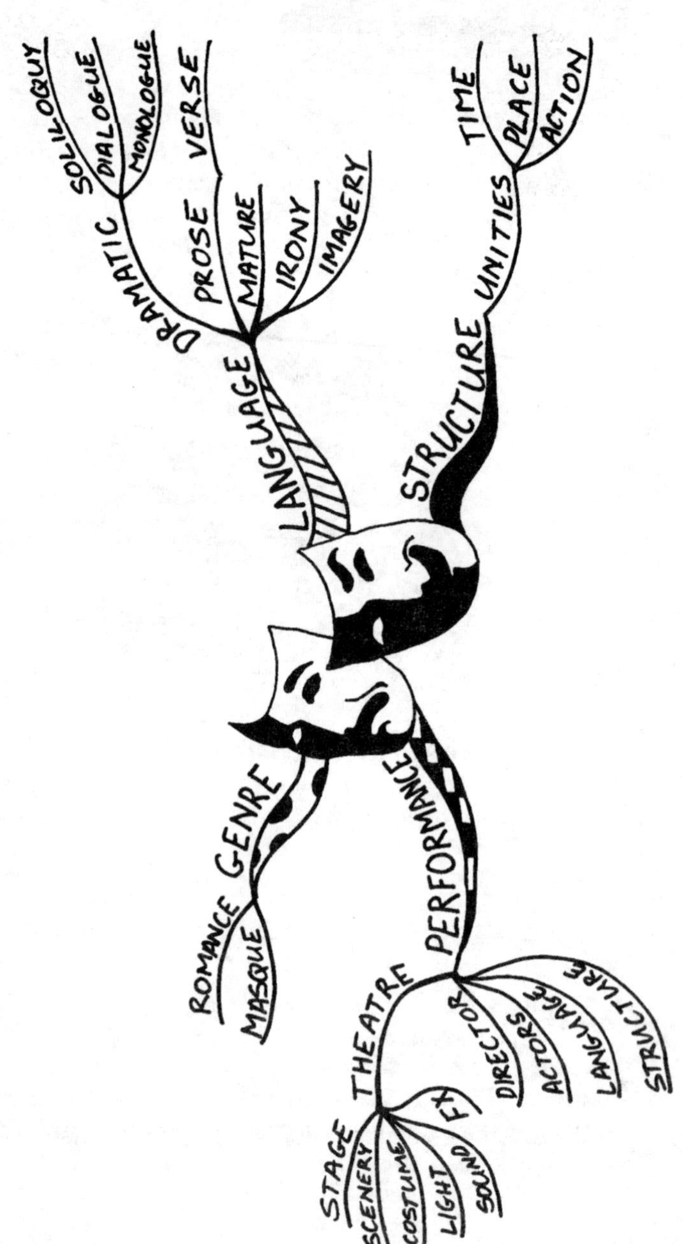
LANGUAGE
DRAMATIC
SOLILOQUY
DIALOGUE
MONOLOGUE
PROSE
VERSE
MATURE
IRONY
IMAGERY
STRUCTURE
UNITIES
TIME
PLACE
ACTION
GENRE
ROMANCE
MASQUE
PERFORMANCE
THEATRE
STAGE
SCENERY
COSTUME
LIGHT
SOUND
FX
DIRECTOR
DIRECTORS
ACTORS
LANGUAGE
STRUCTURE

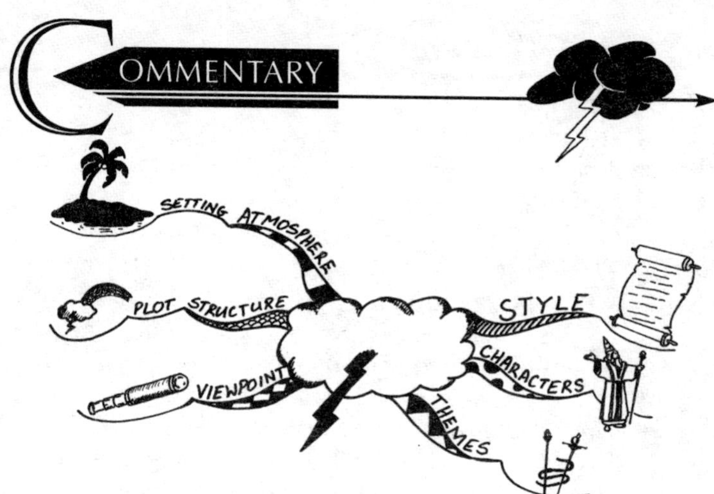

The Commentary looks at each scene in turn, beginning with a brief preview, which will prepare you for the scene and help with revision. The Commentary comments on whatever is important in the scene, focusing on the areas shown in the Mini Mind Map above.

ICONS

Wherever there is a focus on a particular theme, the icon for that theme appears in the margin (see p. x for the key). Look out, too, for the 'Style and language' sections. Being able to comment on style and language will help you to get better marks.

You will learn more from the Commentary if you use it alongside the play. Read a scene from the play, then the corresponding Commentary section – or the other way around.

QUESTIONS

Remember that when a question appears in Commentary with a star ✪ in front of it, you should stop and think about it for a moment. And **do remember to take a break** after completing each exercise!

Act 1, scene 1

- A storm at sea.
- Sailors struggle to save ship
- Passengers interfere, Boatswain curses them.
- Shipwreck.

A STORM AT SEA

The play begins on a ship at sea, in the middle of a storm (the tempest which gives the play its title). The stage directions call for the noise of thunder and lightning effects. The storm has been staged in different ways over the years but it is intended that the play starts with a bang, involving sight and sound, and making a big impression on the audience.

SAILORS STRUGGLE TO SAVE SHIP (LINES 1–7)

The Master (Captain) of the ship tells the Boatswain (second-in-command, pronounced 'Bosun') to hurry up and get the sailors working to avoid the ship running aground. ✪ Can you find three different ways of saying 'hurry up' in lines 3–7?

PASSENGERS INTERFERE/BOATSWAIN CURSES THEM (LINES 8–45)

Some passengers come out. They are obviously worried about the storm, but the Boatswain becomes annoyed with them. ✪ Look at Alonso's first words (line 8) and suggest why the Boatswain might take offence at them. The Boatswain tells the courtiers to stay in their cabins, as they are in the way and stopping the sailors doing their work. Gonzalo reminds the Boatswain who is aboard (Alonso, the King of Naples) but the Boatswain replies that the storm does not take any notice of whether someone is a king or not. He tells Gonzalo to stop the storm himself if he can, otherwise to go to his cabin and get ready for disaster. ✪ The Boatswain speaks very roughly to the courtiers. Do you think he is right to do so?

There is a saying, 'He that is born to be hanged, will never be drowned.' Gonzalo, obviously rather annoyed with the Boatswain, jokes that the sailor's face looks like the face of a man destined to die by hanging. He takes comfort from this: if the saying is right, the Boatswain (and therefore, Gonzalo hopes, everyone else) will escape drowning.

SHIPWRECK (LINES 46–60)

Sailors bring the news that the ship is lost. The boatswain asks *must our mouths be cold?* He means 'do we have to die?'. Many productions also show him sharing a drink with the other sailors at this point, giving his words the additional meaning of 'do we have to die without a warming drink?' This is an interpretation, suggested by Antonio's later accusation that the sailors are all drunkards. It is an example of how Shakespeare's words can give clues to performance. Remember that there are many ways to interpret Shakespeare's plays. You should always give evidence from the text to back up any interpretation.

STYLE AND LANGUAGE

Bad language. We might expect the Boatswain to curse a lot. Many low status characters in Shakespeare do. But when Sebastian and Antonio – who are high status courtiers – join in, it is a bit surprising. ✪ Look at lines 36–40 and 49–52. What do they tell you about the characters of Sebastian and Antonio? Do you think the Boatswain deserves their curses?

Nautical language. Shakespeare uses accurate nautical language throughout the scene to describe what is happening and what the sailors are doing. The ship is near the island, being blown towards the shore and risks running aground (*Fall to't yarely, or we run ourselves aground*). The sailors try to turn the ship away from the shore to avoid this but they need plenty of room in the sea to do this (*Blow till thou burst thy wind, if room enough*). The boatswain gives various orders to try and turn the ship away from the island (*Take in the topsail ... Down with the topmast ... Bring her to try with main-course*). But all efforts fail, the ship runs aground and begins to break up (*We split, we split!*). At the end of the scene we are left not knowing what happens to the people on board.

Act 1 scene 2

- ◆ Miranda asks Prospero to calm the tempest.
- ◆ Prospero tells Miranda the story of their past.
- ◆ Ariel tells Prospero about the shipwreck.
- ◆ Ariel asks for his freedom.
- ◆ Prospero and Miranda visit Caliban.
- ◆ Ariel leads Ferdinand to Prospero and Miranda.
- ◆ Miranda and Ferdinand meet and fall in love.
- ◆ Prospero imprisons Ferdinand.

MIRANDA ASKS PROSPERO TO CALM THE TEMPEST (LINES 1–15)

Miranda suspects that her father has caused the storm and asks him to stop it. This scene shows Miranda's compassion and **empathy** (experiencing emotion along with another): *O I have suffered/ With those that I saw suffer!* In contrast to Miranda's gushing emotional outburst, Prospero's reply is clipped and unemotional. He assures her that no one has been hurt.

✪ Prospero's lines (13–15) could be played coldly or gently. How would you advise an actor to play them?

PROSPERO TELLS MIRANDA THE STORY OF THEIR PAST (LINES 16–186)

Prospero decides to tell Miranda why he has caused the storm. He reminds her that she knows nothing about her past and, taking off his magic robe, prepares to tell Miranda her life story. Prospero speaks to his magic garment, addressing it as *my art*. It is as if his magic power were contained in the robe and, in laying it aside, he becomes a mere human again. Prospero asks Miranda if she remembers anything about her life before she came to the island, bearing in mind that she was not yet three years old. Miranda says that she can remember being looked after by several women, but nothing more. Prospero begins to tell her their history:

- Twelve years ago, he was the Duke of Milan.
- His brother, Antonio, managed the state so that Prospero could concentrate on his studies.
- Antonio learned how to make people do what he wanted.

- While Prospero was busy with his books, Antonio began to be ambitious for more power.
- Antonio plotted with one of Prospero's enemies, the King of Naples, offering him money and influence if he would help Antonio to become the Duke of Milan and get rid of Prospero.
- One night, the king's men took Prospero and Miranda away from Milan and, instead of killing them, set them adrift at sea in a rotten boat.
- Gonzalo helped Prospero and Miranda by supplying them with provisions, including Prospero's precious magic books.
- Prospero and Miranda arrived on the island where they have lived ever since.
- Fate has brought Prospero's enemies within reach, and he must act now or never.

Prospero is kind and affectionate towards Miranda in this scene. He uses her name, and other endearments (*my daughter, my girl, wench*) frequently. He tells her that she kept him going through all his troubles: *O, a cherubin/ Thou wast that did preserve me.* Miranda is respectful and obedient toward her father. She does everything he tells her and shows a real interest in the story. Nevertheless, Prospero continually reminds her to listen carefully, as if she is not paying attention.

✪ Look back over the story Prospero tells Miranda about their past (lines 16–186). How many times does he remind her to pay attention? How does she respond? Why do you think Prospero does this? The story Prospero tells is very emotional for him. Perhaps he is just nervous, and wants to make sure that Miranda understands everything. Or perhaps the story makes him so angry that he can't help taking it out on Miranda. Or, Miranda's attention could be wandering during Prospero's long explanations.

Another possibility is that Prospero puts Miranda into a kind of trance when he tells her to sit down in line 32, and that this makes her sleepy, needing to be kept alert every now and then, and finally falling into a deep sleep at line 185. There are many different ways of interpreting Shakespeare's words. As long as you can back up your argument with evidence from the text, you should feel free to suggest your own ideas.

PROSPERO'S LANGUAGE

Prospero has never told Miranda the story of their past. For twelve years he has kept it to himself. Now, finally, he can unload all his feelings. This affects the way that he tells his story. See 'Drama', p. 33, for an analysis of the language Prospero uses.

ARIEL TELLS PROSPERO ABOUT THE SHIPWRECK (LINES 187–237)

When Miranda falls asleep, Prospero resumes his role as magician by putting on his magic robe again. He summons Ariel, who enters immediately. Ariel appears in a light and happy mood, subservient to Prospero. He is established immediately as a creature of the air and the supernatural world. He can: *fly, dive into the fire, ride/ On the curled clouds*. This will be contrasted later with Caliban, who is associated with the earth and the natural world. Prospero asks Ariel if he has carried out his instructions, and Ariel tells him, *To every article*. Ariel always completes his tasks quickly, exactly and without mistake, a fact of which he reminds Prospero when asking for his freedom later in the scene.

Ariel joyfully describes the mayhem he caused on board the ship. The fiery light he created could have been based on the freaky weather phenomenon, known as St Elmo's Fire, which can happen during storms at sea. Shakespeare may have come across this idea in one of the accounts of the Bermuda shipwreck (see 'Background' in this guide), which describes this event:

> *..an apparition of a little round light, like a faint star, trembling, and streaming along with a sparkling blaze, half the height upon the main mast, and shooting sometimes from shroud (sail) to shroud.*

Prospero is delighted with Ariel and shows his affection: *My brave spirit!, Why, that's my spirit*. He asks Ariel if the people on board are safe. Earlier in the scene he assured Miranda that they were. ✪ Was he telling her more than he really knew at that time, to put her mind at ease? Who was actually in control of the tempest, Prospero or Ariel? Although many productions show Prospero commanding the storm, the text tells us that Prospero told Ariel what to do and Ariel performed the magic.

Look at Ariel's lines in this section to see how many times he says 'I', followed by some action he has performed; e.g. *I boarded, I flamed, I left cooling, I dispersed,* etc. Prospero may be a powerful magician, but much of his power comes from being in charge of Ariel and the other spirits on the island. Keep an eye out for which magical feats are Prospero's and which are performed by Ariel and the spirits.

STYLE AND LANGUAGE

Ariel's language is full of movement. It is hard to read it without imagining Ariel moving around, acting out his words. These are some of the features of his language:

- blank verse
- short phrases and sentences, creating the sensation of speed
- lots of verbs, often magical actions: *I flamed, I'd divide*
- hyphenated words, creating vivid, new meanings: *sight-outrunning, up-staring.*

ARIEL ASKS FOR HIS FREEDOM (LINES 237–305)

Prospero commends Ariel for his work but tells him there is more to do. He spells out the time frame of the play, which is between 2pm and 6pm, and tells Ariel that they must spend the time *preciously*. This tells us that the action of the play is limited to a very short space of time – little more than the time it takes to perform. Ariel reminds Prospero that he has served him well, making no mistakes, and asks Prospero to free him. Angry, Prospero turns on Ariel. Almost immediately, all affection is gone and Prospero is threatening Ariel. He accuses the spirit of being ungrateful and recounts the story of Sycorax.

- Sycorax, the wicked witch, was banished from Algiers to the island.
- Ariel was her servant but she punished him for refusing to carry out her commands, by imprisoning him in a cloven (split) pine tree.

- Ariel remained in the tree for twelve years, during which time Sycorax died.
- Caliban, her son, was the only other inhabitant of the island.
- When Prospero arrived on the island, he released Ariel.

This helps the audience to understand more about the background to the story. Now we know how Prospero and Miranda came to the island, and who was there when they arrived – Caliban and Ariel. We also know that both Caliban and Ariel are enslaved to Prospero. Prospero threatens to confine Ariel in an oak tree if he complains again. Ariel seems frightened of Prospero. He answers Prospero's furious questions with humble, one-line answers, like a child being told off. Ariel promises to do what Prospero asks and not to complain again. Prospero promises Ariel that he will be free in two days. Ariel is instantly grateful, childlike and eager to please again.

Master and servant

? Pick out words or phrases that Prospero and Ariel use in speaking to each other. Make a chart showing who speaks them, and whether they convey good (e.g. kind) or bad (e.g. angry) feelings. Examples: *brave spirit; noble master; dull thing.*

? Speak the words and phrases aloud using different tones; for example: affectionate, angry, resentful, fearful, rebellious, moody. Which tones do you think best suit the characters of Prospero and Ariel?

this is the longest scene in the play, so take a few minutes off before meeting Caliban

PROSPERO AND MIRANDA VISIT CALIBAN (LINES 306–74)

Prospero wakes Miranda and suggests that they go to see Caliban. Although she does not like him, Prospero reminds her that they depend on Caliban to wait on them and do their dirty work. He summons Caliban, addressing him as *Thou earth,* contrasting him with Ariel's airy qualities. As Prospero curses Caliban from outside his cave, Caliban shouts from within, refusing to come out. While they are waiting, Ariel appears, dressed up as a water nymph. Prospero praises his disguise: *Fine apparition! My quaint Ariel,* his words contrasting sharply with those that follow, to Caliban: *Thou poisonous slave ... come forth.*

Caliban eventually appears, cursing Prospero. Prospero punishes him for this by promising to give him cramps and pains. Caliban ignores this and recounts his view of the relationship between Prospero and himself:

- Caliban says that the island rightfully belongs to him, and that Prospero has stolen it from him.
- He remembers that when Prospero first came to the island, he was kind to Caliban and taught him many things.
- In return, Caliban gave him his love, and knowledge of the island.
- Now Caliban regrets it because Prospero has made him a slave when he used to be his own master.
- Prospero has forced Caliban to live in a cave, and kept the rest of the island from him.

Prospero accuses Caliban of lying, and gives his point of view. Prospero says that he was kind to Caliban, until Caliban tried to rape Miranda. Caliban does not deny this; rather, he laughs and says that he wishes he had done it, so the island could have been filled with little Calibans. ✪ Do you think that his attitude shows an evil nature, or does he have a different view of sexuality from that of Prospero?

At this point, Miranda says that Caliban is not capable of learning to be good. She taught him to speak her language, but this could not hide his evil nature. Miranda's words are aggressive, unlike the passive language she used earlier. Although in the original play these lines (351–62) are Miranda's, for a long time they were given to Prospero, and still are in some texts. ✪ Do you think they are more characteristic of Prospero, or can you understand why Miranda might speak to Caliban like this?

Caliban's retort to Miranda is: *You taught me language, and my profit on't/ Is, I know how to curse.* What does this mean? Caliban could be agreeing with Miranda, that all he is capable of is evil, that all language has given him is the ability to curse. Or he could be speaking rebelliously, saying that Miranda and Prospero may have thought they could tame him by teaching him to speak, but that he is still his own person, and he will use their language as a weapon against them. ✪ What do you think?

Prospero tires of Caliban's complaints and threatens him with further punishments if he does not do his work. Caliban becomes fearful (as Ariel did earlier in response to Prospero's threats) and agrees to obey. He says that Prospero's magic is even greater than the power of his mother's god.

One view of Caliban is that he reflects what happened to the natives of a country colonized by Europeans. Prospero can be seen as the colonist who arrives on the island and declares himself master of all who live there.

ARIEL LEADS FERDINAND TO PROSPERO AND MIRANDA (LINES 375–406)

Ariel enters, singing. Ferdinand follows him, strangely drawn by the music that he can hear. Ariel is invisible to him. Ferdinand believes that the music is supernatural, saying that it is for *some god o'th'island,* but he is not frightened. Rather, he seems comforted by it, explaining how the music calmed the storm and his own grief over his father (who he thinks died in the shipwreck). Ariel's first song is about the calming of the storm, and the second song tells how Alonso has undergone a *sea-change/ Into something rich and strange.*

MIRANDA AND FERDINAND MEET AND FALL IN LOVE (LINES 407–58)

Prospero reveals Ferdinand to Miranda, who is instantly besotted with him. She cannot believe that something so perfect could be human. Similarly, when Ferdinand sees Miranda he thinks she is a goddess. Prospero is full of glee – he secretly planned for the two young people to fall in love. In his excitement, he promises to set Ariel free. He repeats this promise several times during the scene. ✪ Find the places where he does this.

Ferdinand speaks to Prospero and Miranda and tells them that he is now the King of Naples, since he saw his father shipwrecked. He mentions that two of the people who died in the wreck were *The Duke of Milan/ And his brave son.* He means Antonio, of course, but who is the son? There is no character either in the scene on board ship, or later in the play, who fits this description. Some people say that it is a remnant of an earlier version of the play, when Shakespeare planned to include this character. ✪ Do you find mysteries like this annoying, or do they add to your enjoyment of the play?

Prospero, to himself, remarks that the *Duke of Milan/ And his more braver daughter* (himself and Miranda) are here to prove Ferdinand wrong. Even though Prospero wants Ferdinand and Miranda to fall in love, he speaks roughly to Ferdinand, explaining to the audience that he does not want him to think that Miranda is too easily won, or he might not value her. Prospero accuses Ferdinand of being a usurper, and of attempting to steal the island from Prospero – of being, in fact, like Antonio. Ferdinand denies this and Miranda tries to defend him.

PROSPERO IMPRISONS FERDINAND (LINES 459–500)

Prospero threatens to imprison Ferdinand. Ferdinand tries to draw his sword to defend himself and Prospero puts a spell on him to stop him moving. Miranda again stands up for Ferdinand. No longer the obedient daughter, she has transferred her affection to Ferdinand and is willing to defy her father for him. You can tell from Prospero's words that Miranda is physically trying to stop her father hurting Ferdinand: *Hang not on my garments!*

Prospero becomes very angry with Miranda and says he will tell her off or even hate her if she goes on. He calls her a fool for loving Ferdinand, when she has only met him and Caliban. He says that, compared to other men, Ferdinand is a Caliban. He means that there may be many better men than Ferdinand.

His words could also mean that there is something of Caliban in Ferdinand – his sexual desire for Miranda. This feeling is echoed later in the play when Prospero continually reminds Ferdinand to control his lust. Miranda claims that she is satisfied with Ferdinand. Ferdinand agrees to obey Prospero, as long as he can see Miranda once a day.

✪ Why does Prospero want Miranda and Ferdinand to fall in love? Why does he go to so much trouble to pretend that he disapproves?

Test yourself

? **Who, what, why, when, where?**

A Where did Prospero and Miranda come from?
B What is Prospero's rightful title?
C When did Prospero and Miranda arrive on the island?
D Who betrayed Prospero to gain power?
E Why were Prospero and Miranda not murdered?
F What happened to them instead?
G Who gave them provisions?
(Answers at end of Commentary, p. 74.)

? How a character looks affects how the audience thinks of him or her. This is particularly important for the characters of Caliban and Ariel. Because these are non-human (Ariel is a spirit), or half-human (Caliban's father is said to be the devil), they have been presented in many different ways. Caliban has been portrayed as a monster, with fins and scales, as a hairy wild man, and as a gentle giant. Ariel has been a woman with fairy wings, an elfin boy and a near-naked man. Talk about how physical appearance affects your understanding of characters in a production you have seen.

? What are your first impressions of Ariel and Caliban? Brainstorm words to describe them, movements or gestures they might make, voices they might use. Add sketches of what you think they might look like.

meet the shipwreck survivors – after a break

Act 2, scene 1

- ◆ Gonzalo tries to cheer up Alonso. Sebastian and Antonio make fun of Gonzalo.
- ◆ Alonso is grief-stricken because he thinks Ferdinand is dead.
- ◆ Gonzalo describes his perfect world.
- ◆ Ariel puts everyone except Sebastian and Antonio to sleep. They plot to murder Alonso.

GONZALO TRIES TO CHEER UP ALONSO (LINES 1–100)

Gonzalo tries to convince Alonso that they are lucky to be alive. The king, grief-stricken because he thinks Ferdinand is dead, does not want to listen to him and tells him to be quiet. Sebastian and Antonio mock Gonzalo, playing on his words, and laughing at how talkative he is. Gonzalo knows that Sebastian and Antonio are making fun of him, but he ignores them. He even returns pun for pun: *dollar/dolour* (lines 18–19), showing that he is no fool, but able to be witty as well. Gonzalo and Adrian argue that the island offers everything they need to survive. Sebastian and Antonio can only see the bad points of the island. This reflects their corrupt view of life.

We learn that the party is returning from Tunis, where the marriage of Alonso's daughter to the King of Tunis had taken place. The conversation about *widow Dido* (lines 72–96) is full of classical references and can seem hard to understand. There are two ways of making sense of this section:

- read it through aloud, concentrating on the mocking tones of Antonio and Sebastian and not worrying too much about all the references
- use the footnotes in a good edition of the play and a dictionary of mythology to help you understand all the references to Dido, Aeneas, Tunis and Carthage.

ALONSO IS GRIEF-STRICKEN (LINES 101–38)

Alonso regrets the journey, because now he has lost his daughter and his son too. Francisco tries to comfort him, saying that he saw Ferdinand swimming strongly after the wreck and that this means he could have reached the shore.

Sebastian, on the other hand, deliberately tries to make Alonso feel worse, saying that it is all his fault that Ferdinand is dead, because he made his daughter marry the King of Tunis, against her will and against the advice of his courtiers. This is an example of a political marriage, made for the benefit of the state, rather than for love. The marriage of Ferdinand and Miranda will also be a political marriage, the union of Milan and Naples, but theirs will be based on love as well.

GONZALO DESCRIBES HIS PERFECT WORLD (LINES 138–81)

Gonzalo talks about what he would do if he were the king of the island. His vision of a perfect world echoes an idea put forward by Michel Montaigne, a French philosopher, in an essay called *Of the Cannibals* (see Background, p.1). Montaigne described some of the values of so-called uncivilized societies – equal rights, free love, shared property, no work – and expressed the view that these societies were better than some European cultures. Gonzalo's vision uses some of these ideas.

Sebastian points out the fault in Gonzalo's argument – that everyone is supposed to be equal, but Gonzalo has set himself up as the king. Gonzalo admits that he was talking nonsense, but says that he did it to give Sebastian and Antonio an opportunity to poke fun. ✪ Look at lines 166–181. Do you think that Gonzalo gets the better of Sebastian and Antonio, or do they make him look a fool?

SEBASTIAN AND ANTONIO PLOT TO MURDER ALONSO (LINES 182–320)

Ariel enters playing music. He is invisible to everyone, but soon, Gonzalo, Adrian and Francisco fall asleep. Then Alonso says he is sleepy. Antonio offers to guard him while he sleeps.

Once Alonso is asleep, Antonio suggests that, if they murdered Alonso, Sebastian would be King of Naples. Sebastian slowly gets the picture and agrees to the plan. However, just as they are about to do the deed, Ariel sings in

Gonzalo's ear to wake him. Gonzalo wakes, sees Antonio and Sebastian with swords drawn and shakes the king awake. Antonio and Sebastian explain the situation away, claiming that they heard the sound of wild animals and were trying to protect Alonso.

STYLE AND LANGUAGE

Even though Sebastian and Antonio do not fall asleep in this scene, their conversation is full of imagery relating to sleep, dreams and the imagination. This could just be a game between them, based on the fact that everyone has fallen asleep around them, or it could be that they are both affected by Ariel's spell as well and are in a trance-like state. Antonio tells Sebastian that his *strong imagination* sees *a crown dropping* on Sebastian's head. Sebastian jokes that Antonio is speaking in his sleep. This could be because he does not want to admit to himself that Antonio is suggesting they murder his brother. Alternatively, there could be something in Antonio's behaviour that makes Sebastian think he is in a trance. This is another example of how the meaning can alter depending on how actors interpret the scene.

This conversation has been compared to the way Lady Macbeth persuades Macbeth to murder Duncan. Antonio uses similar techniques to convince Sebastian to try to murder Alonso. He

- suggests to Sebastian that he is missing a once-in-a-lifetime **opportunity**: *Thou let'st thy fortune sleep;*
- appeals to Sebastian's **ambition**: *What a sleep were this/ For your advancement!*
- suggests the idea using **colourful language**, painting a vivid picture, without actually saying the words, 'kill' or 'murder': *We were all sea-swallowed...to perform an act/ Whereof what's past is prologue; what to come/ In yours and my discharge;*
- outlines a **practical plan**: *Here lies your brother...Whom I with this obedient steel...can lay to bed forever.*

Try this

? Antonio's language is rich in **imagery**. Look at the examples below and add any more that you can find. Read the words aloud, repeating them in different ways (e.g. as an echo, whisper, question, shout, or any other way). What sense impressions (pictures, sounds, smells – even feelings and tastes!) do they bring to mind? Does the image change when you say the words in different ways? Draw pictures to help you remember each phrase.

as a cat laps milk
sea-swallowed
he that sleeps here, swims
a crown dropping
ebbing men
obedient steel

take a short break before some comic relief

Act 2, scene 2

- Caliban curses Prospero and describes the punishments he has received.
- Trinculo finds Caliban hiding under a cloak, and joins him to shelter from the storm.
- Stephano finds them and mistakes them for a monster with four legs.
- Trinculo and Stephano are reunited.
- They all get drunk.
- Caliban offers to serve Stephano.

This is a humorous scene, full of cases of mistaken identity, singing and drunkenness. The humour comes from the performance as much as the words and you will understand the scene better if you can see it on the stage or on video.

CALIBAN CURSES PROSPERO (LINES 1–17)

Caliban said earlier that the only thing he had gained from learning language was that he knew how to curse.

This scene opens with him cursing Prospero, even though he knows that the spirits can hear him and that he might be punished for it. He says he *needs must curse.* ✪ Does this support Miranda's argument that Caliban is naturally bad and cannot be taught to be good, or does it suggest that Caliban feels so badly treated that he must get his own back somehow – or is there some other explanation?

Caliban says that Prospero sets the spirits upon him for every little thing he does wrong and describes some of the punishments. ✪ How many different punishments are there? When Trinculo enters, Caliban mistakes him for a spirit and hides under his cloak.

TRINCULO FINDS CALIBAN HIDING UNDER A CLOAK (LINES 18–38)

Trinculo worries that another storm is coming. He discovers Caliban and marvels at his strange appearance and smell. He says that if he took Caliban to England, people would pay money to see him, and comments: *When they will not give a doit to relieve a lame beggar, they will lay out ten to see a dead Indian.* (lines 30–1). This could be a reference to the fact that some explorers brought back natives of other countries and exhibited them at fairs and shows.

STEPHANO MISTAKES THEM FOR A MONSTER (LINES 39–89)

Stephano enters, drunk and singing. He discovers Caliban and Trinculo under the cloak and there is a great deal of comedy made of the fact that he thinks it is a monster with two mouths and four legs. At the same time, Caliban thinks that the spirits are tormenting him. Stephano gives Caliban wine, saying that it will *give language* to him. Later, in Act 3, scene 2, we will see that too much wine has taken away Caliban's ability to speak!

TRINCULO, STEPHANO AND CALIBAN GET DRUNK (LINES 90–152)

Eventually, Trinculo and Stephano recognize each other and there is further comedy as they are reunited. Caliban begins to get drunk and believes that Stephano is a god, who carries *celestial liquor.* Stephano encourages Caliban in his mistake, telling him that he comes from the moon. Caliban promises to show Stephano the island and to serve him instead of Prospero. Trinculo says that Caliban is a *ridiculous monster* to believe that drunken Stephano is a god. Critics have argued that Caliban's willingness to serve a new master shows that he is a born slave, not able to think for himself. Others say that it shows his trusting nature and his lack of ambition – he just wants his freedom. ✪ What do you think Caliban's behaviour in this scene says about his character?

STYLE AND LANGUAGE

Caliban begins the scene speaking in verse (lines 1–14). His curses and his description of Prospero's punishments are vivid, poetic and full of natural imagery. Again, at the end of the scene (lines 146–50 and 153–8), he uses poetry to describe the delights of the island. Caliban's poetry shows that, far from being an unteachable savage, he is a sensitive character with a real feeling for language and nature. Stephano and Trinculo, on the other hand, speak in prose, as lower status characters in Shakespeare usually do. Caliban also lapses into prose when speaking to these characters, reflecting the mundane nature of their conversation.

PARALLELS IN THE SCENE

1 Stephano's relationship with Caliban parallels Prospero's treatment of Caliban when he first arrived on the island:

- Prospero taught Caliban language. Stephano's downmarket version of Prospero's learning comes in a bottle – he says that the drink will give Caliban language.
- Prospero was kind to Caliban, who then shared his knowledge of the island happily. Caliban believes Stephano is being kind to him and promises to show him the secrets of the island, too.

2 The way that Stephano and Trinculo treat Caliban parallels the way that New World explorers sometimes took advantage of the natives of the countries they colonized. They told them stories to impress them (such as pretending to come from the moon), gave them alcohol and brought them home to be exhibited at fairgrounds. Both Trinculo and Stephano think about the profit that could be made out of Caliban. Only Trinculo has the wit to criticize the practice, commenting that people will not give money to someone in need (*a lame beggar*), but will pay to see a dead person exhibited.

Test yourself

? Draw a Mind Map with Caliban in the centre. Add branches showing everything that happens to him in this scene. Then add further branches showing parallels with the way Caliban has been treated by Prospero, or how New World natives were treated by explorers.

take a break before moving from slapstick comedy to pure love

Act 3, scene 1

- Ferdinand performs the labour Prospero has set him, dreaming of Miranda.
- Miranda arrives and begs Ferdinand to rest.
- Prospero watches as Ferdinand and Miranda declare their love for each other.

FERDINAND PERFORMS THE LABOUR PROSPERO HAS SET (LINES 1–15)

Prospero has given Ferdinand the same task as Caliban – carrying logs. In contrast to Caliban's reluctance to work, Ferdinand is happy to undergo this hard labour, because he thinks about Miranda as he works. The contrast between their attitudes is highlighted even more by the juxtaposition (placing contrasting things next to each other) of Ferdinand's acceptance of his imprisonment with Caliban's rebellious words at the end of Act 2, scene 2:

No more dams I'll make for fish,
Nor fetch in firing
At requiring...
Freedom, high-day, freedom
(lines 165–71)

Ferdinand's speech contains several contrasts; e.g. *baseness/nobly, poor matter/rich ends.* ✪ How many others can you find in this speech?

MIRANDA ARRIVES AND BEGS FERDINAND TO REST (LINES 16–32)

Miranda enters, followed by Prospero who remains throughout the scene, unnoticed by the lovers. Miranda urges Ferdinand to rest for a while. She is openly disobeying her father, believing him to be *hard at study*. This recalls the behaviour of Antonio, years ago, who took advantage while Prospero was wrapped up in his books. Miranda even offers to carry the logs for Ferdinand. Miranda has been brought up away from society and is not held back by ideas of how young girls should and should not behave. She offers to do manual labour, and when Ferdinand says it would be a *dishonour* for her to do it, she replies: *It would become me/ As well as it does you.*

FERDINAND AND MIRANDA DECLARE THEIR LOVE (LINES 32–98)

Prospero is pleased that Miranda and Ferdinand are falling in love and his comments during the scene reflect this. His presence reminds us that it is he who is in control of the love affair, even though the lovers do not know this.

Miranda tells Ferdinand her name, admitting that she is disobeying Prospero to do so. Ferdinand praises Miranda. He says that he has known many women, but that they were all flawed. In his opinion, Miranda is perfect. Miranda, in return, says that she does not know any other women except herself, nor any *that I may call men* other than her father and Ferdinand (ruling out Caliban as not being worthy of being called a man). Despite this, she says that she would not want anyone but Ferdinand. Miranda again shows her innocence of society's conventions by being direct and honest. She openly asks Ferdinand if he loves her, admits that she cannot hide her own feelings, and asks him to marry her. Ferdinand does not seem to be put off by her boldness and agrees.

STYLE AND LANGUAGE

Ferdinand's clever love poetry includes:

- **P**lays on words: when Miranda tells him her name (which means 'wonderful'), Ferdinand plays on the meaning, with *admired* and *admiration* (because to *wonder* and to *admire* are similar in meaning)
- **A**lliteration: e.g. *perfect/peerless*
- **I**magery: e.g. *patient log-man*
- **R**epetition: e.g. *you, O you*

You could remember these techniques using the mnemonic, **PAIR.** ✪ Can you find other examples of these techniques in Ferdinand's language?

Miranda's language is simpler and more direct. When she tries to speak less plainly (lines 79–81) she gets in a muddle and admits that the more she tries to hide her feelings, the more they show. She admits that she is more comfortable with *plain and holy innocence* than *bashful cunning*.

The contrast between freedom and bondage, seen in the end of the last scene and the beginning of this, is carried over as a theme in the language used by Miranda and Ferdinand. Ferdinand says that his heart is at Miranda's service and that he is her slave. Miranda says that if Ferdinand will not marry her, she will be his servant. Their words imply that love is a type of bondage, but one that they will enter willingly. Ferdinand says that he is as willing to marry her as a prisoner in bondage would be to have freedom.

Act 3, scene 2

- Stephano, Trinculo and Caliban are still drinking.
- Trinculo makes fun of Stephano and Caliban. Stephano threatens to punish him.
- Ariel gets Trinculo into trouble.
- Caliban outlines a plan to kill Prospero.
- Ariel hears and plans to tell Prospero.
- The others follow Ariel's music.

This scene brings us back down to earth after the delicate love scene between Ferdinand and Miranda. Caliban, Stephano and Trinculo, in their drunken state, provide earthy comic relief. Later in the scene, the comic sub-plot to murder Prospero is outlined. This reflects the main theme in the play, the usurpation of Prospero by Antonio.

TRINCULO MAKES FUN OF STEPHANO AND CALIBAN (LINES 1–34)

Stephano enters declaring that they will not drink water until they have finished all the wine. He seems a bit carried away with the idea of himself as master and Caliban as his servant. Caliban, unused to alcohol, is virtually speechless. In Act 2, scene 2, Stephano said that drink would give Caliban language. Now he admits that it has taken it away: *My man-monster hath drowned his tongue in sack* (line 11). Stephano's gift to Caliban (wine), like Prospero's (language), has turned out to be a bad thing.

Trinculo is drunk as well but seems to have a clearer view of things. He makes fun of Stephano and Caliban, picking up on the silly things that they say. Caliban complains that Trinculo is mocking him and Stephano threatens to punish him if he continues.

ARIEL GETS TRINCULO INTO TROUBLE (LINES 35–80)

Caliban asks Stephano to listen again to his request. Caliban tells Stephano of how Prospero stole the island from him and suggests that Stephano could kill him and become lord of the island. As Caliban talks, Ariel pretends to be Trinculo and keeps interrupting, saying *Thou liest.* Caliban and Stephano become angry with Trinculo, Stephano beats him and they send him away.

CALIBAN OUTLINES A PLAN TO KILL PROSPERO (LINES 80–109)

With Trinculo out of the way, Caliban explains his plan:

- Prospero sleeps in the afternoon
- Stephano, first having seized his magic books, can kill him
- Stephano will be able to have all Prospero's goods
- Miranda will make him a good queen.

Caliban tells Stephano three times that it is important to take Prospero's books before he attempts to kill him. Caliban knows that with his books Prospero will be able to defend himself; without them he is as powerless as Caliban. Caliban also states that all the spirits hate Prospero. ✪ Do you think this is true, even of Ariel?

Caliban's speech mirrors that of Antonio in Act 1, scene 2, when he tried to persuade Sebastian to kill Alonso. Both characters use language cleverly to convince the other person to do what they want. Stephano agrees to Caliban's plan and apologizes to Trinculo.

ARIEL OVERHEARS AND PLANS TO TELL PROSPERO (LINES 110–47)

Ariel hears Caliban and Stephano plotting to kill Prospero and says that he will tell his master. Caliban, happy that Stephano has agreed to the plan, asks for a song. Stephano and Trinculo begin to sing and Ariel plays the tune. Stephano and Trinculo are frightened by this music coming out of the air, but Caliban tells them not to be afraid – the island is full of strange noises, but they are not harmful. They all follow Ariel's music.

Caliban's words to Stephano: *Be not afeard...* demonstrate again that he is in tune with the natural world, and able to express its beauty with elegance and vivid imagery. ✪ Compare this speech with Caliban's description of Prospero's punishments (Act 2, scene 2, lines 1–14). There, he described how nature, controlled by Prospero, could be cruel. Here, he talks about the gentle magic that is a part of the island. Caliban's words could make you pity him, as he describes the music that soothes him to sleep, and the *riches* he dreams about. In Caliban's life, he has only sleep and dreams to give him pleasure, the rest is work and torment.

Act 3, scene 3

- Alonso and his courtiers are lost on the island.
- Prospero causes a magic banquet to appear.
- Ariel accuses Alonso, Antonio and Sebastian of their sins against Prospero.
- Alonso is overcome by guilt and threatens suicide.
- Antonio and Sebastian threaten to attack the spirits. The others try to stop them.

ALONSO AND HIS COURTIERS ARE LOST ON THE ISLAND (LINES 1–17)

Gonzalo and Alonso are tired after wandering around the island. They have been unable to find Ferdinand and Alonso finally accepts that he is dead: *He is drowned...Well, let him go.* It has been said that their wandering through the *maze* represents a spiritual journey for Alonso, as he first suffers the loss of Ferdinand and then learns to repent for his sins. Antonio and Sebastian, on the other hand, do not change at all. They are still intent on murdering Alonso, and resolve to do it that night.

PROSPERO CAUSES A MAGIC BANQUET TO APPEAR (LINES 18–52)

This is an opportunity for a big stage spectacle. ✪ How would you present the banquet? Read the stage directions before lines 17 and 19 and create a mental video of what the sequence would look like, including your own interpretations of the following directions: Prospero, on top, invisible; several strange shapes; a banquet; dance; gentle actions of salutations; inviting the king to eat; they depart.

The courtiers are amazed at the spectacle and talk about other travellers' tales they have heard. They swear that now they have seen this, they will believe those unlikely stories. Gonzalo comments that the *strange shapes* must be people of the island, and that, although they are of *monstrous shape,* they seem to be *more gentle* and *kind* than many of their own kind. This again recalls Montaigne, the philosopher, who introduced the idea that savages could be 'noble'. Prospero agrees with Gonzalo, commenting that *some of you there present/ Are worse than devils.* ✪ Who does he mean?

Sebastian is the first to suggest that they eat the banquet, showing that he is a man controlled by earthly desires, including hunger as well as ambition. Alonso is frightened to eat the magical feast but Gonzalo persuades him and they prepare to eat.

ARIEL ACCUSES ALONSO, ANTONIO AND SEBASTIAN (LINES 53–93)

Suddenly the scene changes. Ariel appears, dressed as a harpy, and the banquet disappears. A harpy is a mythical creature with the head of a woman and the body of a bird. In mythology, harpies were the **personification** of storm winds, and were also used to give out divine punishment. Both references are relevant here.

Ariel accuses Alonso, Antonio and Sebastian of being *three men of sin.* When they draw their swords, Ariel ridicules them. He says that he and his spirits represent Fate and it is as useless to try to hurt them as it would be to attack the winds or the seas. Ariel continues to use natural imagery as he recounts how Prospero and Miranda were wrongly exiled from Milan, and how this *Incensed the seas and shores.* In Act 1, scene 2, the sea and the wind were described as feeling *pity* for Miranda and Prospero and here again, nature is seen to be in sympathy with them. Here, as in other Shakespeare plays, a crime against a ruler and a brother is considered to be a crime against nature, and this is why nature is in sympathy with the victims. Ariel tells Alonso that as punishment, his son has been taken away and that only repentance and leading a good life from now on can save them.

Ariel disappears and Prospero praises his performance and that of the spirits. He comments that all his magic is working and that his enemies are now in his power.

ALONSO, OVERCOME BY GUILT, THREATENS SUICIDE (LINES 95–102)

Alonso is horrified by the vision of the harpy. The emotional 'O' sound, followed by the repetition of *monstrous*, shows the great guilt that he feels. He repeats the idea that nature is in sympathy, saying that he heard the *billows*, the *winds* and the *thunder* accusing him. He believes it is his wrongdoing that has caused Ferdinand's death and, overcome by remorse, he threatens suicide.

ANTONIO AND SEBASTIAN THREATEN THE SPIRITS (LINES 102–9)

Unlike Alonso, Antonio and Sebastian are not in the least repentant. Their reaction is to take up their swords and run after the spirits, threatening to fight them. Gonzalo asks Adrian and Francisco to run after the other three to prevent them doing anything impulsively.

Reviewing Act 3

? The illustrations opposite review what has happened in Act 3. Look back through the act to find a suitable quotation to use as a caption for each picture. Write it in the space below each picture.

? Who said the following? (Answers on p. 74)

A *Be not afeard, the isle is full of noises.*
B *You are three men of sin.*
C *Hence, bashful cunning,/ And prompt me, plain and holy innocence.*
D *O, it is monstrous: monstrous!/ Methought the billows spoke and told me of it.*
E *Fair encounter/ Of two most rare affections.*

take time off before the spectacula masque

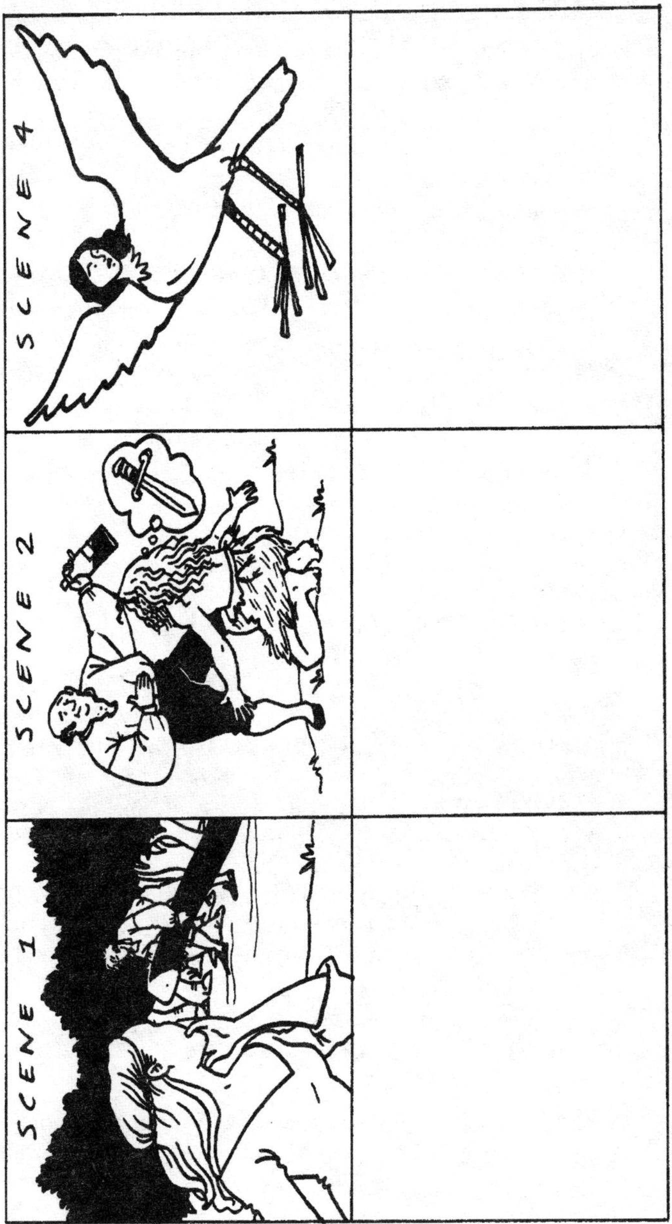
SCENE 1
SCENE 2
SCENE 4

Act 4, scene 1

- Prospero agrees to the marriage of Miranda and Ferdinand.
- Ariel and the spirits perform a masque to celebrate the engagement.
- Prospero remembers the plot on his life and stops the show.
- Prospero and Ariel lay a trap.
- Stephano and Trinculo fall for the trap.

PROSPERO AGREES TO THE MARRIAGE (LINES 1–59)

Prospero tells Ferdinand that his punishments were a test of his love for Miranda. He agrees that Ferdinand has passed the test and offers his daughter to him. He warns against sex before marriage. Ferdinand promises that he will not allow lust to overcome his honour. He is able to use his soul (reason, logic and honour) to control his body (desire, need and physical pleasure). ✪ Compare this to Caliban's uncontrolled expression of sexual desire.

Prospero commands Ariel and the spirits to perform a *vanity*, a theatrical treat for the young couple. Ariel agrees happily. His rhyming answer (lines 44–8) is light and tripping, suited to Ariel's happy nature, but it finishes with a curious line: *Do you love me master? No?* ✪ Do you think Ariel is playful when he says this, or is he desperate for affection and approval? What about Prospero's answer: *Dearly, my delicate Ariel?* Does he mean this, or is he just brushing Ariel off?

Prospero suddenly reminds Ferdinand again to control his lust (lines 51–4). ✪ Why do you think he does this? Does he see Ferdinand and Miranda doing something they shouldn't, or is he just paranoid?

ARIEL AND THE SPIRITS PERFORM A MASQUE (LINES 59–138)

Prospero tells everyone to be quiet and the masque begins. It is sometimes difficult for students to grasp this part of the play. If you can remember two things about the masque, it will help you to see why it is important to *The Tempest*.

1 **The masque is a spectacle**. Masques were short plays, involving music, dance, spectacular effects and scenery. They were usually performed at court and were very expensive affairs. Prospero uses his command over the spirit world to stage this show in honour of Miranda and Ferdinand. This demonstrates Prospero's power and provides an opportunity for a sensational piece of theatre entertainment.

2 **The masque is a symbol**. The masque uses characters from mythology to symbolize themes in the play:
- Ceres – goddess of the fertile earth (where we get the word **cereal**)
- Juno – queen of the heavens, her month (**June**) considered most favourable for weddings
- Iris – messenger of the gods, travelled between heaven and earth on a **rainbow**
- Venus – goddess of **love** and beauty
- Cupid – Venus's son, representing **sexual love**.

The masque begins with Iris describing the bounty of the earth over which Ceres reigns. This is a symbol of all the good things that will come from the wedding of Ferdinand and Miranda. Ceres replies to Iris with many references to rainbows: *many-coloured messenger, each end of thy blue bow, rich scarf*. A rainbow is a symbol of peace after a storm. Iris links earth and heaven in a perfect union, just as the marriage of Ferdinand and Miranda will unite Milan and Naples.

Ceres asks if Venus or Cupid will be present, referring to the story of how she lost her daughter Persephone to the god of the Underworld (a Greek myth), and blaming them. Iris says that they will not be there and reports how they tried to make Miranda and Ferdinand indulge in sexual activity before marriage but failed. Juno appears and together with Ceres they sing blessings on the marriage of Miranda and Ferdinand. The fertile imagery that they use symbolizes both earthly riches and the promise of children that will result from the marriage.

The masque represents Prospero's vision of a perfect world – the union of nature and civilization, without any of the bad bits. Iris, the rainbow, links the earth (body) with the heavens (soul). Venus and Cupid (uncontrolled sexual desire) are banned from the occasion. Unfortunately, Prospero's vision turns out to be an illusion, when it is interrupted by thoughts of what is missing from his perfect world – greed, lust and violence.

PROSPERO STOPS THE SHOW (LINES 139–63)

In the middle of the masque, Prospero remembers that Caliban, Stephano and Trinculo are planning to kill him. He stops the show and sends the spirits away. Ferdinand and Miranda comment on how angry he seems. Prospero notices that Ferdinand seems worried and reassures him, saying that it was only a play they watched, which was insubstantial and impermanent – like life itself.

STYLE AND LANGUAGE

Prospero's lines from *Our revels now are ended* to *our little life/ Is rounded with a sleep* describe the temporary nature of a theatre production. The speech is full of theatrical imagery, referring to actors, scenery and theatrical devices. ✪ Use the footnotes in a good edition of the play to help you identify all the theatrical references. The speech is a metaphor for the impermanence of human life, as Prospero makes clear at the end, with:

We are such stuff
As dreams are made on; and our little life
Is rounded with a sleep.
(lines 156–8)

Prospero starts the speech saying *Be cheerful* to Ferdinand, but his words seem to reflect quite a grim view of the world, saying that nothing we do will last. ✪ Do you find his words depressing, thoughtful or something else?

PROSPERO AND ARIEL LAY A TRAP (LINES 164–93)

Prospero calls Ariel and tells him that they must get ready to confront Caliban. His words are warlike: *We must prepare to meet with Caliban* – and Ariel calls him *commander* in return. Ariel tells Prospero about Caliban, Stephano and Trinculo – how drunk they were and how he led them into a swamp with his music. Prospero instructs Ariel to fetch some gaudy things (*trumpery*) with which to tempt the three conspirators. He reflects that Caliban cannot be civilized: he is *a born devil, on whose nature/ Nurture can never stick.* Prospero says that he has taken great pains to try to educate Caliban, and all in vain.

Thinkers in Shakespeare's time were interested in the 'Nature–Nurture' debate – the question of how far our personality traits are simply inherited, and how far they can be changed by upbringing and social influences. ✪ What do you think about this? From reading *The Tempest,* what do you think Shakespeare's views were?

STEPHANO AND TRINCULO FALL FOR THE TRAP (LINES 193–263)

Ariel returns with the items of gaudy clothing and Prospero tells him to hang them over a line. Prospero and Ariel hide and wait for Stephano, Trinculo and Caliban. They arrive, complaining about the fact that they are soaked and stinking from being in the swamp, and that they have lost their bottles of wine in the pool. Caliban reminds Stephano why they are there – to murder Prospero – and Stephano sets his mind to the task, saying: *I do begin to have bloody thoughts.* ✪ Imagine how this line could be delivered in either a serious or a comic way. Which do you think would be better?

When Trinculo notices the clothes, he is immediately interested. Caliban tells him it is *trash* and tells him to leave it alone. Then Stephano joins Trinculo in dressing up in the clothes. Caliban is angry with them for being so trivial and urges Stephano to *do the murder first.* Caliban is frightened that Prospero will wake and punish them. When Trinculo encourages him to play with them, he says: *I will have none on't.* Throughout the scene Caliban retains a seriousness and dignity in contrast to Stephano's and Trinculo's childishness.

Notice how, as in the previous scenes where they appeared together, Caliban speaks in verse while Stephano and Trinculo use prose. ✪ What does this tell you about his character?

While Stephano and Trinculo are wasting time, Prospero and Ariel set some spirit dogs on them, and the three conspirators are chased off stage. Prospero sends Ariel after them to inflict more punishments on them. Prospero's words reflect the satisfaction he must feel, having all his enemies at his mercy (lines 259–61). He again promises Ariel his freedom soon. Remember that in Act 1, scene 2, Prospero said that he would set Ariel free if he helped him to carry out all his plans today. At many points during the play, Prospero has kept Ariel going with the idea of winning his freedom. ✪ How would you advise the actor playing Ariel to respond to Prospero's promises?

Magnificent masque

- ? The masque in Act 4, scene 1 is supposed to be a spectacle involving music, dance and special effects. Storyboard a section of a modern music video, using words and ideas from the masque (lines 60–117).
- ? Prospero goes through several changes of mood in this scene. Sketch faces to suggest his different moods and, underneath, write something which he says while in that mood.

take a break before the final act

Act 5, scene 1

- ◆ Prospero and Ariel discuss the fate of Alonso and his followers.
- ◆ Prospero promises to renounce his magic.
- ◆ Alonso and his followers are brought in and Prospero judges them.
- ◆ Prospero tells Alonso about Miranda and Ferdinand. Alonso and Gonzalo bless their marriage.
- ◆ The Boatswain explains the strange things that have happened to the ship and the mariners.
- ◆ Caliban, Stephano and Trinculo are reprimanded.
- ◆ Prospero promises to tell all. He frees Ariel.
- ◆ Prospero asks the audience to help complete the story.

This is the final scene of the play, where all the plots are resolved:

- Prospero becomes Duke of Milan again.
- Alonso begs Prospero's forgiveness.
- Antonio and Sebastian are held at bay, but are not repentant.
- Alonso and Ferdinand are reunited.
- Miranda and Ferdinand are blessed by Alonso.
- Caliban is repentant.
- Stephano and Trinculo are reprimanded.
- Ariel is set free.

PROSPERO DECIDES THE FATE OF ALONSO AND HIS FOLLOWERS (LINES 1–32)

Prospero is pleased that his plan is working. Ariel tells him that Alonso and all his followers are imprisoned in the lime grove. Alonso, Antonio and Sebastian are in a trance. Gonzalo, Adrian and Francisco are mourning them. Ariel says that, if he were human, he would feel pity for them. Some people say that even though Ariel is not human, he still feels compassion for the courtiers. ✪ Do you agree? This encourages Prospero to announce that he intends to forgive them. He says that, although he is still very angry with them, he will be merciful. He uses his *nobler reason* to control his *fury*.

PROSPERO PROMISES TO RENOUNCE HIS MAGIC (LINES 33–57)

Prospero calls on the spirits, describing all the magical feats they have helped him to do, and promises to renounce this power over them. Prospero's lines are a kind of spell. The words are very similar to those said by the witch Medea in *Metamorphoses* by the Roman poet Ovid. Some of Shakespeare's audience would have recognized this reference and been impressed by the connection. Because *The Tempest* is probably Shakespeare's last play some people have suggested that Prospero's renunciation of his magic represents Shakespeare's farewell to the stage. Prospero's promise to *break my staff and drown my book* could be seen as Shakespeare giving up imaginative writing. ✪ Do you agree with this interpretation?

PROSPERO JUDGES ALONSO AND HIS FOLLOWERS (LINES 58–134)

Ariel brings in Alonso and his followers. The stage directions are very detailed here. ✪ Read through them and create a mental video of the entrance. While the courtiers are still charmed, Prospero speaks to them, one by one, pronouncing his judgement on them. He is affectionate to Gonzalo, joining him in shedding tears. He accuses Alonso and Sebastian of cruelty towards himself and Miranda. For Antonio, he reserves the worst insult of all: *unnatural.* Yet at the same time, he says he will forgive him.

Prospero asks Ariel to get his hat and rapier – symbols of civil power – and he changes out of his magic garments and into his Duke's clothes. This transformation symbolizes Prospero's renunciation of his magic and his regaining of the dukedom from Antonio.

Prospero sends Ariel to get the mariners, again promising him his freedom soon. As the courtiers come out of their trance, Prospero reveals himself to them. Each reacts differently to him. **Alonso** renounces the dukedom stolen from Prospero and repents his wrongs towards him: *Thy dukedom I resign, and do entreat/ Thou pardon me my wrongs* (lines 118–9). **Gonzalo** for once is almost speechless. After only a few words, he is silent for another 80 lines or so. **Sebastian** cries that *the devil speaks in him!* (meaning Prospero). Typically, he sees evil in everything, even in Prospero.

Antonio says nothing. This is perhaps the most interesting reaction, and leaves scope for actors to add their own interpretation of Antonio's reaction. ✪ Why do you think Shakespeare made Antonio remain silent? How would you advise an actor playing Antonio to react to Prospero's words:

> *For you, most wicked sir, whom to call brother*
> *Would even infect my mouth, I do forgive*
> *Thy rankest fault...*
> (lines 130–2)

PROSPERO TELLS ALONSO ABOUT MIRANDA AND FERDINAND (LINES 134–215)

Alonso mourns the loss of his son Ferdinand. Prospero tells him that he has also lost a daughter. This is an example of dramatic irony (where the audience knows more than a character). We know that Alonso's son is alive, and that when Prospero says he has lost a daughter he means that she has fallen in love with Ferdinand. Shakespeare carries on the joke for quite a few lines, before revealing Ferdinand and Miranda playing chess. ✪ How appropriate a game do you think this is this for them to be playing?

Some critics argue that this emphasis on loss reflects a Christian theme – that it is necessary to experience loss before you can find salvation. Both Prospero and Alonso lose something very dear to them, and both change for the better as a result.

Ferdinand and Alonso are reunited happily. The genuine affection between them is obvious. Ferdinand says that the seas have been merciful to have spared his father. This reflects the theme of the whole final act.

Miranda is amazed to see all the courtiers. Having seen so few people before, she is impressed with them. She thinks that a world that contains people like this must be perfect. Her words:

> *O wonder!*
> *How many goodly creatures are there here!*
> *How beauteous mankind is! O brave new world*
> *That has such people in't!*
> (lines 181–4)

are another example of dramatic irony, because we know that the group she is looking at includes three men who have behaved disgracefully. Prospero echoes our amusement with a faintly ironic: *'Tis new to thee.*

Alonso again expresses his repentance by remarking that he will have to ask his new daughter, Miranda, to forgive him. Prospero tells him to stop worrying about past troubles.

With this, we are sure that Prospero and Alonso are truly reconciled. Gonzalo at last finds his tongue and uses it to outline optimistically everything that has happened. Typically, he sees everything as turning out for the good. ✪ Read Gonzalo's summary of the situation (lines 205–13) and think about whether you agree that everything has turned out well.

Alonso blesses Ferdinand and Miranda and curses anyone who does not wish them well: *Let grief and sorrow still embrace his heart/ That doth not wish you joy.* ✪ Is he thinking of anyone in particular when he says this?

THE BOATSWAIN RECOUNTS STRANGE HAPPENINGS (LINES 216–55)

Ariel returns with the Master of the ship and the Boatswain. Gonzalo exclaims that he knew that the Boatswain wouldn't drown, justifying his words in Act 1, scene 1. He accuses the Boatswain of causing God to abandon the ship because of all his swearing and asks if he will curse now. The boatswain answers seriously, without a hint of his earlier rebelliousness, showing that he too has been transformed by his experiences. He reports that the ship has been restored to its original state and that the mariners are all safe after waking from a strange trance.

Alonso remarks again on the strangeness of events and Prospero tells him not to worry, he will explain everything later. Prospero asks Ariel to bring Caliban and his companions to him.

CALIBAN, STEPHANO AND TRINCULO REPRIMANDED (LINES 256–98)

Stephano and Trinculo enter, as full of themselves as ever. Caliban, however, is humble. Like Miranda, he is impressed by the sight of so many people. There are several parallels between Caliban and Miranda: they have both been educated by Prospero; they are 'children of nature' in that their experience is limited to the island; and they are both impressed by humankind.

While Caliban was not taken in by the gaudy clothes in Act 4, scene 1, he is now impressed by the sight of Prospero. ✪ Why do you think he says: *How fine my master is?* Is it the royal clothes, or can Caliban see that Prospero has regained the dignity and power of a duke, or is there some other reason? Caliban has lost all the rebelliousness he had earlier and is now frightened that Prospero will punish him.

Sebastian and Antonio remark that money could be made from Caliban, echoing the thoughts of Stephano and Trinculo when they first met him. This shows that Sebastian and Antonio are only concerned with earthly things. Prospero explains who Caliban is and admits that he is responsible for him: *this thing of darkness, I/ Acknowledge mine.* It has often been said that Prospero is admitting that Caliban represents a darker part of his own nature. ✪ What do you think of this idea?

Stephano and Trinculo explain how they have suffered on the island, and seem repentant. Caliban promises to *be wise hereafter, / And seek for grace.* Actors playing Caliban have interpreted these lines differently. Some play it straight, showing Caliban to be truly repentant. Some speak the lines ironically, as if Caliban is only pretending. ✪ How would you advise an actor playing Caliban to perform these lines?

PROSPERO PROMISES TO TELL ALL, AND FREES ARIEL (LINES 299–317)

Prospero invites the courtiers to stay on the island for one night, and he will explain the story of his life. Then, he will return to Naples with them, for the marriage of Miranda and Ferdinand, after which he will return to Milan: *where/ Every third thought shall be my grave.* ✪ Why does Prospero refer to his grave here? Is he just inviting pity (rather like 'I've not long for this world...'), is he admitting that he has achieved what he wanted to and can now retire contentedly, or is there some other explanation?

Prospero gives Ariel one last task – to make sure that the seas are calm for their return voyage – and sets him free. Prospero's words to Ariel are affectionate but very brief. Ariel does not respond at all. This seems strange after the intense relationship between them. ✪ Imagine how Ariel reacts to Prospero's words. Create a gesture that sums up his feelings.

PROSPERO ASKS THE AUDIENCE TO HELP COMPLETE THE STORY (EPILOGUE – LINES 1–20)

After everyone else has left the stage, Prospero turns to the audience and addresses them directly. It was common in Shakespeare's plays for an actor to step out of role and speak to the audience at the end of the play, asking for their applause. Prospero seems to stay in his role, saying that he must either be confined to the island or go on to Naples. He says that the audience has the power to decide what happens to him. He asks them not to keep him on the island with a spell, implying that it is now the audience rather than Prospero who has magic power. ✪ Is this magic power their imagination? He asks instead for them to release him with their good hands. This could mean that he wants their applause, but also that he is asking them to pray for him. Just as he has been merciful to the other characters in the play, Prospero now appeals to the audience for mercy.

An eventful day ...

? The action of *The Tempest* takes place in one day. At the end of the day, much has changed. Imagine you are Prospero, Caliban or Ariel. Write a diary entry for the day in the voice of your chosen character.

celebrate – you've reached the end

Answers

'Who, what, why, when, where?' (p. 48)
(A) Milan; (B) Duke of Milan; (C) Twelve years ago; (D) Antonio; (E) Because the people loved Prospero dearly; (F) They were abandoned at sea in a wreck of a boat; (G) Gonzalo.

Reviewing Act 3 (p. 62)
(A) Caliban (Act 3, scene 2, line 130); (B) Ariel (Act 3, scene 3, line 53); (C) Miranda (Act 3, scene 1, lines 83–4); (D) Alonso (Act 3, scene 3, lines 95–6); (E) Prospero (Act 3, scene 1, lines 76–7).

TOPICS FOR DISCUSSION AND BRAINSTORMING

One of the best ways to revise is with one or more friends. Even if you're with someone who hardly knows the text you are studying, you'll find that having to explain things to your friend will help you to organize your own thoughts and memorize key points. If you're with someone who has studied the text, you'll find that the things you can't remember are different from the things your friend can't remember – so you'll be able to help each other.

Discussion will also help you to develop interesting new ideas that perhaps neither of you would have had alone. Use a **brainstorming** approach to tackle any of the topics listed below. Allow yourself to share whatever ideas come into your head – however silly they seem. They will get you thinking creatively.

Whether alone or with a friend, use Mind Mapping (see p. vi) to help you brainstorm and organize your ideas. If with a friend, use a large sheet of paper and coloured pens.

Any of the topics below could feature in an exam paper, but even if you think you've found one in your actual exam, be sure to answer the precise question given.

TOPICS FOR DISCUSSION

1. Who is your favourite character in the play? Why?
2. Write down the names of all the characters in *The Tempest* then choose a word to describe each one.
3. Why does Prospero choose mercy rather than revenge?
4. How many different kinds of magic (either real or illusion) can you find in the play?
5. If you were auditioning for a part in *The Tempest*, who would you like to play?
6. Choose a passage from the play that you would read for your audition and make notes about how you would perform the lines.
7. What do you think Caliban and Ariel should look like? Make some rough sketches of each character, adding notes about costume, make-up and physical performance, and giving reasons for your decisions.
8. Draw a map of the island.

HOW TO GET AN 'A' IN ENGLISH LITERATURE

In all your study, in coursework, and in exams, be aware of the following:

- **Characterization** – the characters and how we know about them (e.g. what they say and do, how the author describes them), their relationships, and how they develop.
- **Plot and structure** – what happens and how it is organized into parts or episodes.
- **Setting and atmosphere** – the changing scene and how it reflects the story (e.g. a rugged landscape and storm reflecting a character's emotional difficulties).
- **Style and language** – the author's choice of words, and literary devices such as imagery, and how these reflect the mood.
- **Viewpoint** – how the story is told (e.g. through an imaginary narrator, or in the third person but through the eyes of one character – 'She was furious – how dare he!').
- **Social and historical context** – influences on the author (see 'Background' in this guide).

Develop your ability to:

- Relate **detail** to **broader content, meaning and style**.
- Show understanding of the author's **intentions, technique and meaning** (brief and appropriate comparisons with other works by the same author will gain marks).
- Give **personal response and interpretation**, backed up by **examples** and short **quotations**.
- **Evaluate** the author's achievement (how far does the author succeed and why?)

Make sure you:

- Know how to use **paragraphs** correctly.
- Use a wide range of **vocabulary** and sentence structure.
- Use short, appropriate **quotations** as evidence of your understanding of that part of the text.
- Use the correct **literary terms** to explain how an author achieves effects with language.

THE EXAM ESSAY

You will probably have about an hour for one essay. It is worth spending about 10 minutes planning it. An excellent way to do this is in the three stages below.

1 **Mind Map** your ideas, without worrying about their order yet.
2 **Order** the relevant ideas (the ones that really relate to the question) by numbering them in the order in which you will write the essay.
3 **Gather** your evidence and short quotes.

You could remember this as the **MOG** technique.

Then write the essay, allowing five minutes at the end for checking relevance, and spelling, grammar and punctuation. **Stick to the question**, and always **back up** your points with evidence in the form of examples and short quotations. Note: you can use '. . .' for unimportant words missed out in a quotation.

Model answer and plan

The next (and final) chapter consists of a model answer to an exam question on *The Tempest,* together with the Mind Map and essay plan used to write it. Don't be put off if you don't think you could write an essay as good as this one yet. You'll develop your skills if you work at them. Even if you're reading this the night before the exam, you can easily memorize the MOG technique in order to do your personal best.

The model answer and plan are good examples to follow, but don't learn them by heart. It's better to pay close attention to the wording of the question you choose to answer in the exam, and allow Mind Mapping to help you to think creatively.

Before reading the answer, you might like to do a plan of your own to compare with the example. The numbered points, with comments at the end, show why it's a good answer.

QUESTION

Some people consider Prospero to be a kind and wise magician; others see him as bitter and cruel. What do you think?

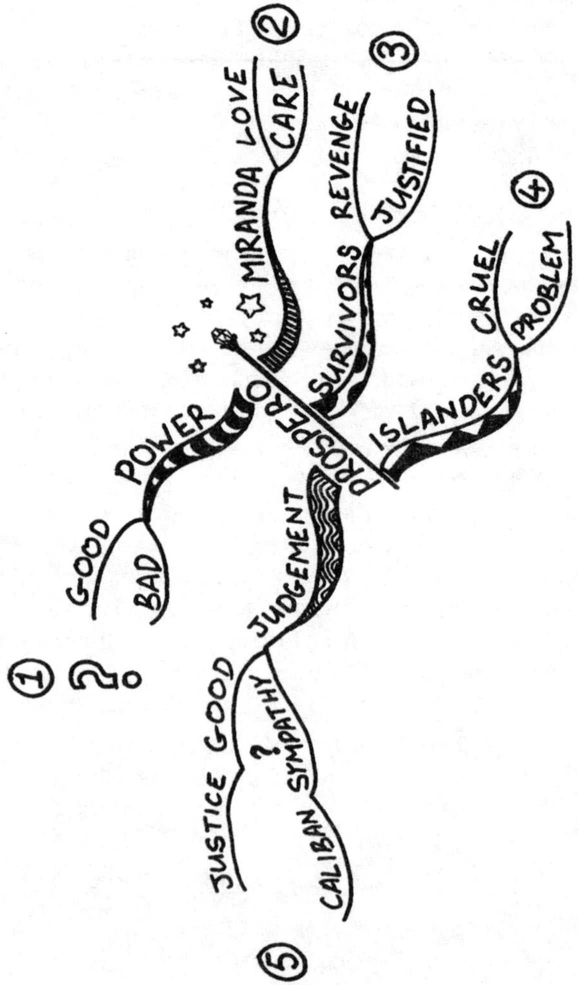

PROSPERO

1 ?
POWER
GOOD
BAD

2
MIRANDA
LOVE
CARE

3
SURVIVORS
REVENGE
JUSTIFIED

4
ISLANDERS
CRUEL
PROBLEM

5
JUDGEMENT
JUSTICE
GOOD
?
SYMPATHY
CALIBAN

PLAN

1. Introduction – Prospero, very powerful, controls action of play. Does he use his power for good? We judge him by how he treats the other characters. Three groups: Miranda, shipwreck survivors and islanders.
2. Miranda – Prospero loves her, only stern because he wants what is best for her.
3. Shipwreck survivors – they are in the wrong, Prospero justified in taking revenge.
4. Islanders (Ariel and Caliban) – Prospero loves Ariel but threatens him. Harsh to Caliban and we feel sorry for him.
5. Conclusion – Prospero basically good and wise. How we judge him depends on how sympathetic we are to Caliban.

ESSAY

From the storm he conjures at the start of the play to the calm seas and auspicious gales that he promises to create to carry the royal parties back to Italy at the end, Prospero controls the action of *The Tempest.*[1] Indeed, his power is so great that some critics have suggested that he is a god-like figure with complete control over the destinies of everyone on the island.[2] Though he is obviously a very powerful magician, whether he is also a kind and wise one is certainly open to debate.

How we judge Prospero depends very much on how we react to the way he treats the other characters in the play. I would suggest that to study this it is best to divide these characters into three groups. First, there is his daughter, Miranda. Then there are the survivors of the shipwreck. Finally there is a group formed by the 'natives' of the island: Caliban, Ariel and the other spirits.[3]

Dealing with Prospero's relationship with Miranda first, it is clear that he loves his daughter. When she questions him about the shipwreck he tells her: 'I have done nothing but in care of thee' and he uses many terms of endearment towards her: 'my girl', 'wench', 'my lady'.[4] On the other hand, he does snap at her several times when he thinks she is not listening to his story, for example: 'Thou attend'st not!' He is also stern with her when she asks for pity on behalf of Ferdinand to the extent of physically pushing her aside, saying: 'Hence! Hang not on my garments.' However, from his asides to Ariel we know that he is only pretending to be angry to make sure that Ferdinand and Miranda really are in love.[5] Miranda is surprised by his harshness but it does not make her doubt him. As she says to Ferdinand:

> 'Be of comfort;
> My father's of a better nature, sir,
> Than he appears by speech. This is unwonted
> Which now came from him.'

How we view Prospero's actions towards the courtiers from Milan and Naples is a little more complicated. Antonio and his accomplices have treated Prospero and Miranda very badly. Prospero vents his feelings about Antonio in the long speech to Miranda referred to earlier. He refers to Antonio as 'thy false uncle' and is clearly amazed and hurt to remember how his own brother wronged him. Prospero's language shows how bitter he feels. The words are almost spat out in a long and urgent narrative. The words are compressed, the imagery is vivid and concise and he often repeats himself.[6]

It is not surprising that he wants his revenge on Antonio, Alonso and Sebastian. Indeed, it could be argued that he allows them to get off lightly since none of them comes to real harm. Sebastian and Antonio are even allowed to go unpunished for their plot to murder Alonso and the good Gonzalo. Prospero's treatment of Stephano and Trinculo is comical rather than cruel. Though their punishments are unpleasant, they do not suffer unduly. The important thing about Prospero's treatment of the travellers from Milan and Naples is that he forgives them in the end. Despite his anger and desire for revenge, he chooses to be merciful, saying: 'The rarer action is/ In virtue, than in vengeance.'[7]

If Prospero has done wrong it is in having spent so much time studying magic that he ignored his responsibilities and allowed himself to be overthrown. Shakespeare's audience might have judged Prospero more harshly than a modern audience. When the play was written (probably around 1611) people believed that the first duty of a ruler was to govern wisely – it was wrong for Prospero to immerse himself in the study of magic and neglect his citizens.[8]

A modern audience is more likely to judge Prospero not for studying magic but for the way he uses it – particularly in his treatment of the islands 'natives': Caliban, Ariel and the other spirits. Shakespeare's audience might not have felt it was wrong for Prospero to use Caliban and Ariel as he does. However, a modern audience might feel uncomfortable when Prospero calls Caliban and Ariel his slaves and rules them with threats. Some directors have even presented the play as a criticism of colonialism where Prospero represents the colonial powers and Ariel and Caliban the native populations.[9]

When he first came to the island, Prospero freed Ariel from a cloven pine tree, where he had been imprisoned by the witch Sycorax. As a result, Ariel is Prospero's servant. Prospero is kind to Ariel, using endearments like 'chick' and 'bird' and praising his work. However, when Ariel challenges Prospero's authority by asking for his freedom, Prospero becomes cruel and vindictive. He calls Ariel a malignant thing and threatens to imprison him in a tree for another twelve years. When Ariel does what Prospero asks, he is kind and affectionate, and in the end, he does fulfil his promise to give Ariel his freedom.[10]

Prospero was also kind to Caliban when he first came to the island. Caliban himself says: 'When thou cam'st first/ Thou strok'st me and made much of me... And then I loved thee.' But Caliban tried to rape Miranda and since then, Prospero has treated him as a slave, calling him: 'hag-seed', 'abhorred slave' and 'malice', and subjecting him to many forms of physical torture. Prospero does seem to regret that all his efforts with Caliban were in vain. He says Caliban is:

> 'a born devil, on whose nature
> Nurture can never stick; on whom my pains
> Humanely taken, all, all lost, quite lost.'[11]

Shakespeare gives Caliban some of the most beautiful poetry in the play, in which he demonstrates that he has a real appreciation of nature, for example:

> 'Be not afeared, the isle is full of noises,
> Sounds, and sweet airs, that give delight and hurt not.'[12]

However, though this does make him more sympathetic, we are never allowed to forget his baser nature: he curses Prospero continually, he wishes he had managed to rape Miranda and he plans a violent end for Prospero, suggesting that Stephano:

> 'with a log
> Batter his skull, or paunch him with a stake,
> Or cut his wezand with thy knife.'

Caliban, perhaps more than any other character, can be interpreted in different ways. Our view of him depends on our own reading of the play, as well as the interpretation in any production we might have seen – which could emphasize his good or evil qualities.[13]

In conclusion, Prospero is a wise and powerful magician. He acts to secure justice and reconciliation, and he is forgiving and merciful at the end.[14] He can be stern and irritable, but he is basically kind, except perhaps in his treatment of Caliban. Thus, how we judge Prospero depends in part on our judgement of Caliban.[15]

WHAT WAS GOOD ABOUT IT?

1 Shows awareness of structure of the play by linking beginning and end thematically.
2 Knowledge of critical opinion and awareness of alternative approaches.
3 Outlines clear structure to essay.
4 Reference to key scene with well chosen evidence from text.
5 Evaluation of character based on words and actions.
6 Awareness of how language conveys state of mind.
7 Confident identification of key theme.
8 Identifies and comments on historical context.
9 Shows awareness of how modern cultural context affects interpretation of play.
10 and **11** Good overview of relationship between characters using well chosen evidence from text.
12 Awareness of Caliban's use of poetry and how this has a positive effect on interpretation of character.
13 Awareness of how performance affects interpretation.
14 Identification of key themes in play.
15 In summary, the essay is a thoughtful personal response to the question, showing insight into character behaviour and relationships; accurate and appropriate use of textual evidence; analysis of language and stagecraft; and awareness of social, historical and cultural contexts.